Income Inequality
and
Economics

Income Inequality
and
Economics

By

Germinal G. Van

Copyright©2019 by Germinal G. Van
All Rights Reserved
Book written by Germinal G. Van
Cover designed by Germinal G. Van
Published by Germinal G. Van and Kindle Direct Publishing
authorgerminalgvan@gmail.com
ISBN: 978-107-82-21160

Printed in the United States

CONTENTS

Books written by the same Author

American Political Culture

Equal Under The Law

Essays On Issues (Volume 1)

Reflection On Identity Politics

The Efficiency of Capitalism

Democratic Socialism On Trial

The Problem Of Egalitarianism

Preface

In order to fully grasp the whole idea of this book, the reader is required to read *The Problem Of Egalitarianism*. Indeed, *Income Inequality and Economics* is a continuity of *The Problem Of Egalitarianism*. In *The Problem Of Egalitarianism*, I gave a philosophical account of why seeking equality as a goal is an individual problem for the citizen, and a collective conundrum for society as a whole. In *Income Inequality and Economics*, I gave an economic and empirical account of why seeking to equalize income is deceptive issue to focus on. The general argument of this book holds that, since inequality is a natural phenomenon, income inequality is then a normative element of any society.

Income inequality is a normal and necessary economic condition because it ensures economic growth. It gives incentives to individuals to seek higher aims in order to advance their condition, and those incentives will evidently stimulate productivity. Moreover, the book argues that if income inequality in America is widening, it is not because the top 1 percent is accumulating all the wealth while the 99 percent remains in poverty, but because the government makes it harder for citizens to expand their purchasing power through government regulations on businesses, government regulation of the price system, the augmentation of inflation, and high taxes on the upper and the middle-classes.

Unlike *The Problem Of Egalitarianism*, which is a book of political philosophy and social theory, this book is a book of economic theory and social philosophy. This book challenges the dominant thought which ascertains that income inequality is the result of man-made exploitation. It attempts to explicate to the reader that equality is, in all righteousness, not superior to inequality despite what the dominant thought wants to make the average man believe.

Germinal G. Van

Introduction

Income inequality is not a notion that needs to be defined. When we look at the words "income" and "inequality"; both words limpidly describe that individuals living in a civil society do not earn the same income for their respective labor. Income and wealth among individuals are drastically unequal. They are unequal because people do not produce the same way, nor the same amount; they do not produce at the same pace; they do not produce with the same intensity nor that they produce under the same terms and conditions. Income and wealth are not the same among members of society because these factors aforementioned play a substantial role in how wealth is produced, and income is earned. For example, the revenues of someone who is hourly paid and that of someone who is salaried; will never be the same. If we take a close look at the labor laws of the United States, according to the Fair Labor Standard Act (FLSA), an employee who works and gets paid hourly is a non-exempt employee, which means that he is entitled to receive compensation for his work when he works overtime.[1] On the other hand, an exempt employee is a worker whose salary is based either monthly or annually.[2] That worker will not receive compensation for his overtime-work because overtime compensation is automatically included within the salary-basis in accordance with the regulations of the FLSA guidelines.[3] So, for example, if a worker is paid $45 an hour and works over 40-hours-a-week and he is non-exempt for overtime compensation, his salary will be nearly close to a $100,000 a year additionally to the overtime compensation he receives; compared to a

---

[1] Coverage under the FLSA. The Fair Labor Standard Act. Department of Labor. https://www.flsa.com/coverage.html.

[2] Ibid.
[3] Ibid.

worker who is paid $85,000 per year and exempt for overtime. In this situation, although both workers are earning sufficiently well to live a good life, there is still inequality of income between the two despite earning good incomes. Consequently, we have to think critically and rationally about inequality rather than emotionally. Is inequality automatically a bad thing? Should people be equal in material wealth by all means? Is inequality not part of human nature and the human condition? If everyone had the same income or the same wealth, how would society look like?

The emotional response to these interrogations about inequality is that, the one who has less than the other is assumed to be automatically worse-off because that person possesses less. The emotional response suggests that having fewer resources imply systematically that one is in a bad situation or condition. If we become specific about income inequality, the emotional response would be that poverty is the cause why the have-nots have either fewer or nothing while the haves are accumulating more wealth, which amplifies their income. The emotional response to income inequality perceives inequality as an impediment and recommends fixing it by righting the wrong, which means ensuring that the have-nots and the haves have the same income if possible because everyone will be better-off if that was the case. The emotional response to income inequality takes grounds in moral premises. Those who perceive income inequality as a conundrum, argue that the have-nots are not to blame as they do not have the adequate resources to improve their condition; therefore, something must be done about it; it shall be rectified. On the other hand, the critical and rational response about inequality in general and income inequality in particular, is that inequality is not a predicament because it is an intrinsic part of the human condition.

The critical and rational response on income inequality suggests that individuals will eventually reach a better social class as their income increases with their professional experience. As social mobility is the main factor that keeps society from remaining stagnated, individuals with low-income eventually move onward higher-income brackets with better skillsets, with more experience in the professional world, and with an increase in their revenues. The critical and rational response sees income inequality simply as a natural process of life. Individuals as well as living beings are not equal. For example, two hyenas may belong to the same species, it does not automatically mean that they are identical or equal. One hyena may have a surplus of physical attributes than the other, which enables it to be more dominant than the other. Should we fix the inequality that is established between the two hyenas because one has fewer physical attributes than the other? The same principle goes for the nature of the human condition. Income inequality in America is real but it is not a curse like some intellectuals may want to make it seem. As it was aforementioned, individuals, at some point in their lives, move up along the income brackets—moving from a lower-income bracket to a higher-income bracket. The top 20 percent of American society is mainly made up of individuals earning over $60,000 a year[4] with an age range of thirty-years-old and above.

In this work of political economy and social theory, the purpose of this book is to simply investigate the factors that contribute to income inequality in America and why it is less of an issue than some intellectuals may want to portray it. If income inequality, on the other hand, has widened, it is simply because government intervention has made it worst. In this book, I endeavored to explain how government, in controlling price and the certain key industries such as education, healthcare, housing, and some parts of the financial sector; has

---

[4] Editors, *How Much Money Do The Top Income Earners Make?* Financial Samurai.   https://www.financialsamurai.com/how-much-money-do-the-top-income-earners-make-percent/. Article. Web.

made it worst to narrow the income inequality gap between social classes. The book invites the reader to fully grasp the mechanism upon those factors which incentivize economic inequality. *Income Inequality and Economics* is a collection of essays that contains ten distinctive political essays. The first essay entitled "The Nature of Inequality" deals with what inequality is about. The essay explains how inequality is an intrinsic element of human nature and how it is needful for the advancement of society. The second essay entitled "Human Capital, Production and Economic Inequality" articulates on the fact that economic inequality is the result of aggregated output. As individuals contribute differently to economic activities, their output is obviously different, which means unequal. The third essay is entitled "Social Mobility." This essay elucidates that social mobility is the quintessential factor that enables the continuity of economic growth and mobility. Without social mobility, economic incentives and development will inevitably be stagnant. The fourth essay is entitled "Government Intervention." The point of this essay is to explicate how government intervention in the economy produces more income inequality among workers than a supposed equalization of income. The effectuation of government regulations makes it harder for individuals to be economically emancipated because their purchasing power is reduced. The fifth essay is entitled "Wealth Redistribution and the Welfare State." This essay elaborates the mechanisms upon which the state uses its coercive power to control the allocation of scarce resources. The use of this coercive power generates inequality of wealth and inequality of income among social classes and individuals. The sixth essay is entitled "Political Leaders and the Art of Resenting." The argument of this essay is to analyze how political leaders of lagging groups such as the Black community or the Latino community, use their authority and influence to preach resentment within these groups. This resentment

24

being spread precludes minority groups from emancipating themselves and continue to blame the more advanced groups for their stagnation. The seventh essay is entitled "Middle-Class and Taxation." This essay illuminates how the middle-class is the one that is the most affected by the system of taxation. Every time the government seeks to create a program, the middle-class is taxed more than the top 1 percent as well as the lower-class. The system of taxation imposed upon the middle-class does enlarge income inequality between individuals. The eight essay is entitled "Unemployment and Inflation." The objective of this essay is to decipher how government intervention in the economy stimulates inflation to increase and how the increase of inflation generates more unemployment. The ninth essay entitled "Personal Behavior and Responsibility" articulates upon the fact that behavior and responsibility are significant variables that play a crucial in the determination of income. If income inequality does exist, it is surely because personal responsibility gets to influence the outcome of the person in the midst of elevating herself socially. The last and final essay is entitled "Political Decisions and Economic Outcomes." This essay seeks to expound how political decisions affect economic outcomes for the worst. This essay aims to enlighten that economic outcomes are better when they are left to the individuals to decide for themselves rather than a bureaucracy deciding on what shall be done economically without having the adequate knowledge to make such decisions.

1.

The Nature of Inequality

Men are not born equal, except before the law. Some people were born with a surplus of skills and abilities that are not mastered through diligence and hard work. They possess these skills because that is the gift that nature has given them. They are able to perform excellently in an endeavor without producing any substantial effort to deliver outstanding outcomes. For example, F.C. Barcelona superstar; Lionel Messi; is considered to be one of the greatest soccer players in the history of the sport because he has accomplished outstanding things that very few players have done. His performances have broken records in many substantive competitions. However, Messi is mainly known to be a naturally gifted player. He did not have to put as twice as much work to deliver the results that we know. On the other hand, Cristiano Ronaldo is also a great player, but he was not born with the same surplus of skills and abilities as Lionel Messi. Compared to Messi, Cristiano Ronaldo had to provide more efforts in order to be able to equate Messi's performances. Some people were born into a family that is materially wealthy. They did not choose their socioeconomic condition, but nature has blessed them enough to have an economic advantage at birth, compared to the other child who did not have that same chance. For example, President John F. Kennedy was extremely lucky to be born from a wealthy family. This wealth he has inherited; enabled him to attend the best schools in the country and facilitated his ascension in the political arena while his 1960 opponent for the presidential race; Richard Nixon; did not have the same economic advantage that President Kennedy had at birth. Nixon had to work twice as hard to equate

Kennedy's social status. And there are other people who were neither born with no particular surplus of skills nor from a rich family. These people were not gifted by the wonders of nature. They had to work twice as much; extremely and diligently hard to achieve success and social elevation. These are those that we call the self-made people. For example; Oprah Winfrey, Bill Clinton, or Bill Gates, have achieved success through their hard work. The point of these arguments and examples, was simply to epitomize that inequality is a natural phenomenon of life that man has no control over whatsoever. The fact that some people were born rich, others poor; some were born with good health, others were born with physical and mental disabilities; some were born with talents, others were born with no distinguished skillsets; demonstrates that inequality, in its own nature, is not a predicament.

What makes the essence of individuality is inequality. Living beings are unequal. By living beings, I entail human beings, mammals, insects, and plants. Even the elements of the earth such as rivers, mountains, forests, and deserts, are not equal. Each of these elements have their own particularities. For example, the Mount Kilimanjaro is known to be the highest mountain on the African continent, but the practicality of life upon this mountain is impossible for human life and animal life to sustain. Inequality, for the fact of the matter, is the factor that ensconces the authenticity of each being. It is because individuals are not equal that they get to be authentic. Inequality between individuals greatly contribute to the way they produce. Since people are not equal, what they produce will certainly not be the same in quality nor in quantity. For instance, two writers in the same literary genre will not necessarily produce the same kind of output. One writer may be a prolific writer and rather focus on producing a dozen of books per year while the other writer may be more concerned with writing one single colossal novel that may encapsulates his entire idea. Based on who the audience is, both writers will be appreciated differently. The prolific writer may be appreciated for his prolificacy while the other writer may gain recognition for having produced a quality book that enshrines a variety of ideas within the same content. It does, by no means, suggest that the prolific writer produced a poor quality of work. A prolific writer may produce a great load of books that are also of great quality. For example, Isaac Asimov, one of the most prolific writers in world, has written more than five hundred books[5] in his lifetime, which were all of great quality works. He was considered to be one of the greatest writers in the science-fiction genre and his excessive output upheld his reputation.

The purpose of inequality is to authenticate originality. If human beings were equal to one another in terms of production, output, and wealth; in what kind of world would we be living in? The reason why innovation exists, it is because the one

---

[5] Seiler, Edward; Jenkins, John H. "Isaac Asimov FAQ," *Isaac Asimov Home Page*. (June 27, 2008).

who produces more has the ability to create new venues in the endeavor in which he has already produced. And this venue will enable others to benefit from that innovation. For example, since Bill Gates has revolutionized the computer industry, he has created new venues in that industry which facilitated the utilization of computerized software by many. Inequality, as it was aforementioned in the introduction, is not inherently an impediment. In fact, it gives a chance to everyone to participate and bring his contribution to all the endeavors that could possibly enhance the human condition. The nature of inequality is meant to advance the subjectivity of the uniqueness of the individual. We, as individuals, feel unique because we possess certain attributes in certain domains that others do not. As rational beings, we are not willing to trade the attributes we have for something less than our value because the attributes that each individual possesses are what determine each individual's value. It deserves to be reiterated that inequality is not intrinsically a predicament to the advancement of the human condition. Inequality and equality are both necessary and respectively essential. On the one hand, inequality is needed because it gives the opportunity to each individual to bring his attributes into the participation of a particular endeavor. On the other hand, equality is necessary to ensure that everyone does have the opportunity to pursue his self-interest under the legal boundaries of the rule of law. In speaking of equality, it is important to emphasize on what kind of equality we are talking about. What is necessary is equality of opportunity; access to opportunities within the rule of law; not equality of outcome.[6] Since the human condition is based on inequality, equality of outcome is simply impossible to achieve and, therefore, impossible to be established as a practical principle. Equality of opportunity is a practical principle.[7] Since human

---

[6] Editors, "Equality of Outcome," *Equality of Opportunity and Education. McCoy Family Center for Ethics in Society.* Stanford University.
[7] Mason, Andy, "Equal Opportunity," *Encyclopedia Britannica.* Article History.

beings are fundamentally unequal, the only circumstance upon which they are equal though, is before the law. The rule of law is the factor that ensures that every individual has the same opportunity to use his attributes for the better. However, equality of opportunity also means that each individual is held responsible for his action before the law. It signifies that it is the responsibility of the individual to make rational and consequential choices regarding what he intends to pursue.

Now the great question in this essay which spurs my intellect is to know when does inequality become a problem. In simple and contractionary words; if inequality is inherently not an issue; then when does it become a conundrum? Inequality becomes a problem when it is believed that political power will deliver economic salvation. As this assertion seems quite ambiguous, it suggests in simple words that inequality becomes a problem when individuals begin to believe that political power is the force that will deliver equitable outcomes for differences already embedded between and within people. This question has been answered but the answer has not been yet elaborated. The elaboration of the response to this question is reserved to be developed in the sixth and tenth essays of this book.

2.

Human Capital, Production, and Economic Inequality

When we speak about raw materials, we generally refer to the subsoil assets such as gold, silver, diamond, bauxite, manganese, oil, uranium; to food crops such as cocoa, coffee, cotton, rice, wheat, corn, rubberwood...etc. It is true that these natural resources are raw materials in the sense that they have not yet been transformed into a finished product. In reality, these natural resources have no intrinsic value unless human activity uses them to advance its condition. It is the quest for the advancement of the human condition that determines the value of natural resources. That being said, the real and true raw material is not the natural resources, but the knowledge of man. It is the knowledge of man that we informally, and somewhat colloquially, call *human capital*. Human capital is an intangible asset, a set of collective resources possessed by individuals and groups within a given population.[8] These resources include all the knowledge, talents, skills, abilities, experience, intelligence, training, judgment, and wisdom possessed individually and collectively, the cumulative total of which represents a form of wealth available to nations and organizations to accomplish their goals.[9] As it was previously indicated, human capital is the first raw material of any given prospective production. Without human capital, the transformation of any given natural resource into a finished product can practically not occur.

---

[8] Huff, Richard, "Human Capital," *Encyclopedia Britannica*, Article. History.
[9] Ibid.

Human capital is the fundamental element of human production and human productivity. It is our activity that brings value to the material we use. The utilization of different materials that we use in order to create capital, derives from our knowledge, and precisely through education. When the human brain is conditioned to perform in any domain, it is because man has acquired the knowledge and developed the necessary skills that facilitate access to the information regarding that domain before performing within it. The main difference between rich and poor nations is based on human resources, i.e. human capital. For example, Japan is one of the richest nations on earth while Niger is one of the poorest ones. Yet Japan has no natural resources, particularly no subsoil assets; while Niger has an abundant set of uranium, bauxite, and oil. How come Niger, a country that is such endowed by natural resources, can be among the poorest nations on the planet while Japan; a country twice bombed by the atomic weapon, with absolutely no natural resources; is among the wealthiest nations on the planet? The answer to this interrogation is, simply, human capital. Although Japan lacks natural resources, it has managed to be economically developed because it has invested its capital in its people. The Japanese government has made of education the first priority of all economic development. Despite all the natural resources that Niger possesses, it is one of the poorest countries in the world because it has not developed its human capital. The Nigerien government has failed to invest in its population in order to properly develop the raw materials that are at their disposal. How did the Nigerien government fail to develop the human capital of Niger? It has failed to create factories that would enable the direct transformation of its raw materials into finished products. Since Niger lacks the factories of transformation, it has to sell its raw materials to other importing countries like Japan at a low price. Those importing countries, then, impose a fixed rate at which they will buy the Nigerien natural resources. The Nigerien government is therefore obliged to concede to the demands of those importing countries since it is those importing countries that have the capital. Nigeriens lack the knowledge to adequately use these scarce resources for the advancement of their own condition. The wealth inequality that is established between Japan and Niger is blatantly striking. According to the data of the OECD and *Trading Economics*, the Growth Domestic Product (GDP) of Japan is at 0.61 percent in 2019,[10] which is the yearly GDP growth in Japan while the GDP of Niger is at 6 percent.[11] In 2013, the natural resources of Niger contributed 12.3 percent of its total GDP, and it is projected that this contribution to GDP will double in 2020.[12]

---

[10] OECD (2019), Real GDP forecast. doi: 10.1787/1f84150b-en (Accessed on 07 August 2019).

[11] "Niger GDP Annual Growth Rate." *Trading Economics*. https://tradingeconomics.com/niger/gdp-growth-annual

[12] Glenn-Marie Lange, Quentin Wodon, and Kevin Carey. *The Changing Wealth of Nations 2018*. World Bank Group. ISBN: 978-1-4648-1046-6. Book.

Colonization is a tool for economic and political development of human capital. This sentence may seem shocking to many because colonization is generally associated with enslavement and oppression of one social or ethnic group over another. It is surely comprehensible and valid. Colonization, whether it was effectuated through direct or indirect administration, has unequivocally harmed the oppressed people who were subjugated to colonial rule; but this wrong deed did however not have an absolute detrimental impact on the colonized. Colonization, in spite of its arbitrary and peremptory nature, is a tool for economic and political development of human capital in the sense that the colonizers possessed the adequate knowledge to develop the human capital of the colonized territories. Among the colonized territories, some have economically and politically developed in becoming prosperous nations such as South Africa, Australia, the United States, Canada, Mexico or Brazil; while other nations such as

Tanzania, Niger, Guatemala, Vietnam, Cuba, Angola, Moldova, Romania, or Bulgaria; became impoverished. Although all these countries mentioned have been former colonies, some became wealthier than others. How come?

During the eighteenth and nineteenth centuries, colonization took place in two succinctly different ways. There was colonization of settlement and colonization of exploitation. The former colonies, which are now rich countries, have undergone a colonization of settlement. It signifies that the colonizers who settled in those territories to make it their own, have whereby established a political system wherein they implement laws by which the oppressed people as well as themselves must abide by. Evidently however, the laws enforced were harsher and more restricted for the oppressed people than for the oppressor. The colonizers have also implemented an economic system in which they create a market and many different venues to expand production. This does not mean in any case, that colonization of settlement was something fabulous where it was great to live in. On the other hand, it has enabled former colonies and its oppressed people to benefit from a system that empower them to increase their living standards. For example, South Africa was subjected to a colonization of settlement wherein the oppressed people, Black South Africans who were the majority, lived in a system of segregation imposed by the White minority European settlers who became South Africans. Despite the horrendous and unjust laws that Black South Africans were forced to abide by during the time of the Apartheid; Black South Africans today have a higher living standard than most Black Africans living in Niger, Sudan, or in the Central African Republic. The system of Apartheid, despite its tyrannical methods, has developed human capital in South Africa politically and economically. Politically because South Africa was one of the first countries in Africa to have an established system of government where the judiciary plays a significant role in the implementation of legal rules and where the legislative branch was more influential than the executive branch. And economically because South Africa was also one of the first market-oriented societies in Africa as well. White South Africans hired Black South Africans to work in factories, and in many other market venues. Black South Africans were able to create businesses which improved employment conditions in townships despite staggering rate of poverty.[13] Today we, all know that South Africa is the most politically and economically advanced nation in Africa. It is the foremost law-abiding nation in the continent. The example of South Africa is, however, not unique to South Africa. The same situation relatively happened in the United States where White Europeans settled in

[13] Ngcamu, Johannes Peter, *The History and Development of Black Entrepreneurship in South Africa*. Faculty of Economic and Management Science at Rand Afrikaans University. (2002). https://core.ac.uk/download/pdf/18219248.pdf. Dissertation.

America and established a political, legal and economic system wherein Black Americans tremendously suffered, but have today a better living standard than most Black people around the world. Canada, Australia, Mexico, and Brazil have also undergone a colonization of settlement. On the other hand, the former colonies that are today considered as poor nations, are those that have suffered a colonization of exploitation. It means that the colonizers did not settle in any of these territories to make it their own and create a new society in these territories. The colonizers only used these territories to extract natural resources without necessarily establishing a legal, political, and economic system in these territories. Former colonies such as Niger, the Central African Republic, Vietnam, Bolivia, Guatemala, or Romania, are poor countries because the colonizers in these territories did not enhance the human capital. They simply used the indigenous populations to extract the raw materials they needed to advance their own economy then left when they could no longer afford having them as colonies. For example, Romania was a former colony of the Soviet Union during the twentieth century. The Soviets did not develop the human capital in Romania. Instead, they simply extracted the raw materials that they needed to advance their own economy and armament. They did not teach the Romanian people the knowledge of using their own natural resources in order to develop themselves if it turned out that the Soviets were no longer able to continue their exploitation. Romania is evidently not the only case in which colonization of exploitation has stimulated more poverty in former colonies that have suffered from it.

Interestingly, certain colonial powers that were historically wealthy, are now some of the poorest nations in Europe; notably Spain and Portugal. Spain and Portugal in the sixteenth century have dominated the Western hemisphere. The Spanish and the Portuguese colonized Latin America, from Mexico all the way to the province of

La Tierra del Fuego in Argentina. They accumulated a staggering amount of wealth in natural resources. But both countries failed to develop the human capital in the territories that they colonized. Except for Mexico and Argentina wherein the Spanish have proceeded to a colonization of settlement, most of Latin American countries have suffered a colonization of exploitation. The Spanish and Portuguese extracted much gold, silver, and other highly-valued minerals to develop their own economy while failing to develop that of their colonies at the time they were colonies. The Spaniards were so wealthy that they did no longer have to actually work to create wealth, which means they did not have to keep developing their human capital. They rest on their laurels and believed that the wealth they accumulated did not need to be multiplied. If Spain and Portugal are among the poorest nations in Europe, it is because of a constant decline in population. Ten years before the discovery of America, the Spanish population was

10,000,000 inhabitants.[14] This number has continuously declined over time. In 1492, after the expulsion of the Jews, the population shrank to 9,800,000 inhabitants; and in the next hundred years, the population of Spain sank to 8,000,000 inhabitants.[15] A possible explication of this gradual decline in human capital is because the transfer of knowledge from one generation to another has not been conveyed. The Spanish and Portuguese failed to produce and reproduce the wealth that they have accumulated through their colonization of exploitation. Wealth is something that evaporates itself if it is not constantly produced, and the Spanish and Portuguese have failed to grasp that concept. For example, if Brazil is more economically advanced than Portugal today, it is primarily and in part, due to the vast migratory wave of immigrants from Germany, Russia, Lebanon, Italy, and also

---

[14] Moses, Bernard, "The Economic Condition of Spain in the Sixteenth Century." *Journal of Political Economy.* Vol. 1; No 4. (Sep. 1893) pp.513-534. Published by the University of Chicago. Article.
[15] Ibid.

Portugal; who have settled in Brazil and developed the human capital there. Like Mexico and Argentina, Brazil did not undergo a colonization of exploitation. In contradistinction to Spain and Portugal, England became, from the seventeenth century to the end of the nineteenth century, the greatest colonial power in the world because it has proceeded by a colonization of settlement. Of course, it does not mean that England has applied a colonization of settlement in every single territory they have occupied. India and Eastern Africa are good examples of colonization of exploitation committed by the British. Nonetheless, unlike the Spanish, the Portuguese as well as the French; the British have settled in most of the places they have occupied. Australia is a perfect example of how the colonization of settlement, although detrimental to the Aborigine peoples, has nonetheless furthered the human capital in that land, which has allowed Australia to become one of the most economically and politically advanced nations on the planet.

Colonization; whether it was colonization of exploitation or settlement; was not a vindictive element for the oppressed people, those who have suffered throughout its deeds. But one positive aspect we can all learn from it is that it has expanded the knowledge of the utilization of scarcity and the concept of human capital.

What makes human capital relevant is scarcity. When resources are scarce, that is when human capital comes into play and does its finest job. The inevitable outcome of the production of human capital is inequality. As human beings are not the same in skills, talents, abilities, capabilities, judgement and intelligence; human capital is undoubtedly used differently by those seeking to advance a particular motive. Economic inequality is simply the result of how human beings allocate scarce resources when they use them and after they have produced them. The most advanced societies are advanced because they utilized their human capital without a central authority planning on how resources would be and should be allocated. As only individuals know their own needs, only them are able to correctly use their capital to maximize the resources that they utilize to produce. Human capital is the ultimate source of any kind of human development.

3.

Social Mobility

The economic development of any society is entrenched in social mobility. Nations that have failed; have done so because they lacked social mobility. The absence of social mobility generates stagnation. The difference of income between individuals is what enables the enhancement of social mobility. As it was aforementioned, people are born differently. Some were born with some advantages and others were not. If we take a close look at social mobility in the United States, we generally observed that all college students who recently graduate, usually start their first professional job as entry-level employees whether they come from wealthy families or working-class families. Evidently, all entry-level jobs do not have the same salaries. Salaries vary according to the industries in which we venture ourselves. According to the Bureau of Labor Statistics (BLS), the median income of a paralegal or legal assistant was $50,940 a year or $24.49 per hour in 2018.[16] Moreover, a paralegal or legal assistant only needs an Associate degree to officially be eligible to work in that field. However, the median salary of a college professor in 2018 was $78,740 per year.[17] When we look at both occupations (legal assistant and college professor), none of the people in these two professions started off with these exact salaries being described. An entry-level paralegal generally starts with $38,000 per year then sees his salary increasing over time with an accumulation of professional experience. College professors generally start with $50,000 a year, then see their

---

[16] Paralegal and Legal Assistants, *Occupational Outlook Handbook*. Bureau of Labor Statistics. https://www.bls.gov/ooh/legal/paralegals-and-legal-assistants.htm. Data.

[17] Professors, Ibid.

salary augmenting over time as well. Since occupations in each venue are not equal, it is evident that incomes will not be the same.

What incentivizes social mobility to occur is the amelioration of practical skills in the field in which we exercise. Practical skills are preponderant because they determine what we worth on the market. An individual with a lower skillset will evidently not earn the salary of someone who has been performing the same task for years. The concept of social mobility practically commences for individuals who are sixteen years of age and above. At sixteen years old, most teenagers start gaining work experience by doing the most low-paid jobs that the market could offer, such as mail telegram deliverer, working in the food industry as servers and waitresses, or selling goods or services on the streets during the summer. These work experiences they are acquiring, enable them to understand how the professional world works. Most teenagers; depend on the area they live and their economic conditions; manage to graduate high school before endeavoring in other ventures. Some start an entrepreneurial career, others pursue a college degree, and other teenagers simply pursue a professional career right after high school. For example, those who pursue an entrepreneurial career at an early age, and those who pursue a professional career right after high school, set themselves in the social mobility mechanism while those who pursue a college degree are not in that mechanism yet. Those who pursue an entrepreneurial or a professional career right after high school have an advantage in terms of work experience and skills practicality over those who pursue a college degree. They will, obviously, move faster from one social bracket to another, mainly a higher social bracket because they have acquired substantial work experience and have improved their skills in the meantime. In the 1960s and 1970s, individuals with only a high school degree were making living wage because having a college degree was not a requirement to be competitive on the labor market and make a decent living. Plumbers, carpenters, and most blue-collar workers were making sufficiently well to easily feed their family. Today, it is undoubtedly more difficult to make a living just with a higher school degree because the augmentation of the minimum wage prevents employers to hire low-skilled workers and those with no college degree. Those, on the other hand, who pursue a college degree, now have the advantage in the mechanism of social mobility because as the minimum wage keeps increasing, most entry-level jobs require applicants to have at least a college degree to thoroughly be eligible to obtain employment. The social mobility that occurs for a recent college graduate is strikingly different than for those who have been working directly since high school, but it depends on where that person obtains a job. For example, a recent college graduate who studied economics or business and who was lucky enough to obtain a job as a junior consultant with a huge consulting firm such as Ernst and Young (EY), KPMG, or Deloitte; will start that job with relatively a median salary of $50,000 per year. $50,000 per year is generally the median income of a middle-class household. The professional worker who started working right after high school though, did certainly not start with a $50,000-a-year salary as an entry-level employee. However, someone who has graduated with a degree in philosophy may have a hard time finding a job in other market venues except in teaching. Though, to teach would imply that, that person will have to go back to school to pursue her graduate studies before being able to make a living while the junior consultant at the EY or KPMG, is already acquiring experience and practical skills, which consequently increase his income significantly.

Those who perceive income inequality as a problem to social ascension, say that social mobility is, in fact, a myth. Their argument is based upon the lack of opportunity. To them, social mobility is a myth because they speculate that people do not have the same opportunities. Opportunity is just one factor in economic advancement.[18] How well a given individual or group takes advantage of existing opportunities is another.[19] Only by implicitly and arbitrarily assuming that a failure to rise must be due to society's barriers can we say that American society no longer has opportunity for upward social mobility.[20] Immigrants who come here in America are initially supposed to have less opportunities available to them than native-born Americans because they are not in their country of origin. They have to adapt and accustom to the language, the culture and the values of the United States. In short, immigrants settling in America are supposed to be disenfranchised, but is quite the opposite that is

---

[18] Sowell, Thomas, *Economic Mobility.* Creators. (2013). https://www.creators.com/read/thomas-sowell/03/13/economic-mobility. Article.

[19] Ibid.
[20] Ibid.

happening. Most immigrants who settle in America and become law-abiding members of American society, generally have a better living standard than native-born Americans from lower social bracket. For example, as we know that having a college degree is paramount for the effectuation and the facilitation for individuals and groups to move from once social class to another, African immigrants are, for the fact of the matter, the most educated immigrants in the United States. Research found that of the 1.4 million Sub-Saharan African immigrants who are twenty-five years old and older, 41 percent have a Bachelor's degree, compared to 30 percent of all immigrants and 32 percent of the American-born population.[21] Of the 19,000 U.S. immigrants from Norway—a country that President Trump reportedly told lawmakers is a good source of

---

[21] Helm, Angela, *African Are the Most Educated Immigrants in US: Report*. The Root. (2018) https://www.theroot.com/africans-are-the-most-educated-immigrants-in-u-s-repo-1822169956. Article. Web.

immigrants — 38 percent have a college education.[22] According to a report released in 2017 entitled *How Sub-Saharan Contribute to the U.S. Economy,* African immigrants were also significantly more likely to have graduate degrees, with 16 percent having a Master's degree, medical degree, law degree or doctorate, compared to 11 percent of the American-born population.[23]

Social mobility is the epitome of income inequality. If we want equality as the motto to promote economic and social advancement, then social mobility will not be able to continue its course. The quest for egalitarian ends leads to social and economic stagnation because it will prevent individuals to bring their potentials and attributes into the participation of economic and social activities. How can development occur if everyone is equal? Egalitarians have argued that social mobility, which is the precursor of the American

---

[22] Ibid.
[23] Ibid.

Dream, is limited to a select few.[24] They argue that the system in place makes it difficult for people born into poverty to get an education and get well-paying jobs.[25] Furthermore, they assert that while social mobility is possible, people who overcome the odds are the exception, not the norm.[26] While their point is not completely unsubstantiated, their argument remains fallacious. Why immigrants — people who come in this country with significant disadvantages such as restricted visas which prevent them from becoming financially emancipated or having the inability to take loans or to even having the inability to have credit scores or social security — do manage somehow to climb the social ladder while the American-born citizens, who have access to public education and government social services; do have difficulties to leave the state of poverty and climb the

---

[24] Crossman, Ashley, *What Is Social Mobility?* ThoughtCo. (2019). https://www.thoughtco.com/social-mobility-3026591. Article. Web.

[25] Ibid.
[26] Ibid.

social ladder like everyone else? Of course, no one chooses his socioeconomic condition at birth. Yet one has the power, the duty and the responsibility to change his economic condition for the better. One possible and plausible explanation for a lower-income-born-American citizen to have difficulty to leave the state of poverty; is the welfare state. In the fifth essay, this answer will undoubtedly be more elaborated. This essay will succinctly explicate how the welfare state is the actual predicament that prevents low-income people to climb the ladder and to embark upon the social mobility train.

4.

Government Intervention

Government intervention in the economy is fundamentally a monumental economic mistake because it complicates the stream of economic and social activities. However, since 1933, this monumental error has been perceived by the court of public opinion; which is not necessarily thoroughly educated on questions of economic policy; as a sort of benefactor to stimulate the economy. When Adam Smith maintained in *The Wealth of Nations* that the government shall not intervene in economic activities, he knew very well why he defended this idea of non-intervention. The reason why the government should not intervene in the economy is simply because, as a third-party, it intervenes into a transaction already established between two parties that conduct their exchange under mutual agreement. The third-party does not have information regarding the conditions under which the transaction between the two parties has taken place. The third-party has no knowledge regarding the sort of agreement which upon the transaction was conveyed. This intervention disrupts the process of the transaction being effectuated, and the outcome of this intervention results into an unequal benefit between the two parties. When a transaction is effectuated between two parties without any form of interference, both parties mutually and equally benefit from that transaction. But when a third-party interferes in the transaction, one party will end up receiving more benefits than the other party, and that inequality in the transaction ends with the third-party benefiting more than the actual two parties involved in the transaction. How come does the third-party ends up benefiting more than the two parties involved in the transaction? Simply because each party involved in the transaction has to pay its due to the third-party which has the duty to "facilitate" and "ameliorate" the process of that transaction. The third-party is the enforcer. Its role is to enforce fairness within the transaction. But fairness is not the real interest of the third-party. It is a mere pretext to justify the enforcement whether it is made subtly or coercively. The real interest of the third-party is to exploit the weaknesses of the losing party in the transaction. When the third-party establishes the rules of the transaction upon which it intervenes, it imposes and enforces regulations against both parties in the name of fairness within the transaction while the third-party, which is the enforcer, does not enforce these regulations upon itself. This is literally how the government operates when it intervenes in the economy and that is exactly the quintessential reason why the government shall not intervene.

1933 was a year of distress when Franklin Delano Roosevelt took office as the thirty-second President of the United States of America. The United States was going through probably the greatest, nonetheless, injurious economic downturn in its history. The Great Depression has, indeed, affected millions of Americans nationwide. Over 20 million people were starving because the economy was collapsing. To fix the economic woes that were severing on the American people, President Roosevelt has decided to stimulate the economy by bringing the federal government into the economy to revitalize it. At first glance, the idea seems good and genuine. President Roosevelt was actually genuine about doing something to save the American people. The economic method that President Roosevelt exerted to stimulate the economy is known as Keynesian economics. This economic theory suggests that the best way to stimulate economic growth is by letting government injecting more money in the economy at lower interest rates so that the masses could borrow more and spend more.[27] Although the idea was good,

---

[27] Chappelow, Jim, "Keynesian Economics," *Investopedia*. (2019).

genuine and well-intended, government intervention in economic activities has serious repercussions over the whole economy. One of the main repercussions of government intervention in the economy is the rise of unemployment. When President Roosevelt injected funds in the economy to reboot it; unemployment, on the other hand augmented, and was slow to shrink. Keynesian economics produces short-term gains and long-term adversarial effects. Government intervention in the economy creates employment on a short-term basis and unemployment on a long-term basis by allowing the government to impose regulations on businesses, which eventually decrease the demand the labor and increase the labor cost.[28] The increase in labor costs makes it harder for private businesses to afford labor demands, and that difficulty in

---

[28] Worstall, Tim, *If you're a Keynesian Then You Must Believe the Minimum Wage Increases Unemployment.* Forbes. (2015). https://www.forbes.com/sites/timworstall/2015/06/13/if-youre-a-keynesian-then-you-must-believe-the-minimum-wage-increases-unemployment/#29024b1cea3d. Article. Web.

supplying labor increases unemployment.[29] For example, unemployment rate under FDR was in the double-digit, precisely at 14 percent after his economic stimulus was implemented.[30] During the first eight years of his presidency, however, unemployment rate was at 18 percent before being brought down to 14.[31] If FDR did not implement an economic stimulus, the economy would have recovered faster. The economy would have recovered faster because the private sector would have regulated prices itself instead of the government, it would have established a price level that the masses could afford according to their purchasing power. The market has a better approach to allocate scarce resources because it determines the

---

[29] Amadeo, Kimberly, *Seven Causes of Unemployment*, The Balance. (2019). https://www.thebalance.com/causes-of-unemployment-7-main-reasons-3305596. Article. Web.

[30] Moore, Stephen, *The Enduring Myth of FDR and the New Deal*. The Heritage Foundation. (2014). https://www.heritage.org/budget-and-spending/commentary/the-enduring-myth-fdr-and-the-new-deal. Article. Web.

[31] Ibid.

prices of the production according to what the consumers want. If the majority of consumers cannot afford the purchase of a given product or service, the entity that provides that product or service will be compelled to reduce its price in order to incentivize demand. When the government intervenes in a transaction, it attempts to regulate prices. It regulates prices by establishing them below that of the market. As government-prices are established below those of the market, products and services are therefore cheaper, so; there is a shortage of supply because there is not enough to supply it to everyone.

President Roosevelt was certainly not the only political leader who used government to control the economy. Most likely every American president has done so. Government intervention has become culturally acceptable by society for the state to interfere in the economy because our political leaders and bureaucrats have made it seem to the ordinary man that economic fairness and income equality can only be achieved if the state gets to regulate the economy as a whole. The state has now been perceived as the remedy to recover from economic recession since the Great Depression in American culture. In Europe as well, Keynesian economics has widespread throughout the continent. For example, the British government has also intervened in the economy in order to restore economic activities in Britain in the 1930s. Another example of government intervention with long-term adversarial effects is the Great Recession of 2008. When the recession of 2008 occurred, President Obama injected funds in the economy for its recovery by stimulating demand — exactly like FDR. This economic stimulus implemented to recover the economy has once again delivered adversarial effects on unemployment; and the cost of labor, which has consequently enlarged the income inequality gap. Unemployment rate under the Obama administration strikingly skyrocketed during the presidency of the first Black President.

Many would say that President Obama inherited from President Bush failed economic policy, so it has to take time for him to fix it. That is the general explication being delivered to the ordinary citizens by the elites of our society. What has, in fact, stimulated the Great Recession of 2008 was the small unknown economic recession of 2001 during the Bush presidency. The economic recession of 2001 which happened from March 2001 to November 2001 resulted in the implementation of the Economic Growth and Tax Relief and Reconciliation Act of 2001 (EGTTRA) by President George W. Bush. This economic stimulus contained a considerable load of regulations that enabled the government to control the price of production, conditions of transactions, and other factors that monitored the economy. Unemployment slightly surged above the nominal rate of 4.5-5 percent, and to be precise, unemployment rate was above 5.7 percent,[32] which means that labor cost was slightly expensive to the effects of the stimulus package. The long-term effect of that stimulus package engendered the Great Recession of 2008. As it was aforesaid, President Obama injected over $700 billion in the economy to stimulate demand. The economic stimulus of President Obama increased the rate of unemployment as well as inflation during his presidency. According to the Bureau of Labor Statistics, it took eight years for President Obama to stabilize unemployment. It took him eight years to bring unemployment back to its nominal rate. When President Obama tool office in late 2008 early 2009, unemployment rate was 7.8 percent in January 2009,[33] That was six months before his economic

---

[32] Amadeo, Kimberly, *2001 Recession, Its Causes, Impact, and What Ended it.* The Balance. (2019). https://www.thebalance.com/2001-recession-causes-lengths-stats-4147962. Article. Web.

[33] Bureau of Labor Statistics (BLS) On Unemployment from 2009 to 2019.

stimulus was injected. His stimulus package was injected in June 2009. In January 2012, almost three years after the economic stimulus was implemented, unemployment rate was at 8.3 percent.[34] It was in late 2016, shortly before President Obama left office that unemployment rate has finally reached its nominal rate. Unemployment rate in December 2016 and January 2017 was at 4.7 percent.[35]

These examples illustrated were to showcase the predicament of government intervention in any form of activity. Politicians advance the rhetoric that government intervention helps while it actually creates more damages. Every time unemployment increases, income inequality also augments because the level of poverty rises. The level of poverty rises because low-skilled workers and other workers cost

https://data.bls.gov/timeseries/LNS14000000?fbclid=IwAR10s52T5 Z0JiM2ZqgCrGmL7fbcAIqp17QVtCZWjPlFRD0svU_riUm4d2cc

[34] Ibid.
[35] Ibid.

too much to the employer. Those who are unfortunately relieved become dependent on the state for financial assistance. They gradually become stagnated if they do not find employment in a near future. Politicians and bureaucrats are the ones in charge of regulating economic activities. They effectuate policies that have detrimental effects on the general population, but they pay no price for being wrong. For the fact of the matter, government is the engine of inequality, it is the precursor that aggrandizes the wealth gap between social classes and individuals. Now the main question is to know why the bureaucrats and politicians; those who create income inequality through their well-intended, nonetheless, adversarial policies; continue to incentivize the ordinary man to embrace those same policies that will eventually harm him? Simply to expand the power of the state. As it was elucidated at the outset of this essay, the state is the greatest beneficiary of any transaction in which it interferes or intervenes. Furthermore, the state wins within the transaction by exploiting the losing party of that transaction. Education, healthcare, and housing have become gradually costly to the taxpayer due to government regulations. For example, the reason why education is expensive in the United States is because of the Higher Education Act of 1965. This legislation allows students with slim financial means to take government loans with lower interests to fund their tuition during their academic career. Once those students obtain their college degree or graduate degree, they end up paying massive debts to the state for the rest of their lives because they cannot go bankrupt since those debts must be paid off to the state instead of a private entity. So, they are obligated, one way or another, to pay off the loans to the government. If the state did not intervene in the education system, those with slim financial means would have had the possibility to make direct arrangements with the school of their choice regarding the payment of their tuition. If the majority of the student body at the university is not wealthy enough to afford expensive tuition, the school will then be compelled to lower its tuition price so that it will have those students who do really want to get their education. In this three-party transaction, the great beneficiary is the state. The state gets to impose the interest rate at which students can take loans and eventually pay-off those loans. The state gets to impose penalties by increasing interest rates on the student's credit score if some payments have not been made. The school, on the one hand, gets to increase its tuition rate every year because the administrators know that students will be taking loans. Students, on the other hand, are the greatest losers of that transaction and the state exploits their vulnerability to expand its power. They are the ones who are doomed to pay-off the state once they have taken student-loans. Students from wealthy families have no problem to afford expensive tuition. But those from working-class families are ill-fated to use those government loans to pursue an education otherwise they cannot get a college or graduate education. Therefore, there is a blatant form of income inequality that has been ensconced from which the state has greatly, nonetheless, preposterously contributed to. The same process goes forth for healthcare and housing. The point is, government intervention complicates the transaction in which it involves itself in. When the government creates a program that ends up failing, bureaucrats create a new government agency to save the previous agency that has been already failing. By proceeding that way, the state does not fix the problem at all, it creates more interference by expanding more regulations. It simply dislocates the problem rather than solving it.

5.

Wealth Redistribution and the Welfare State

The welfare state is surely the system that makes income inequality greater than ever. Despite its good intention to help those in need, to give a shelter to those who have none, the provide food to those who lack the resources to feed themselves; the welfare has, as a matter fact, done more harm than good to those it intended to help. To acutely fathom the concept of the welfare state, it is preponderant to comprehend the idea of the redistribution of wealth and its effects on the socioeconomic condition of everyone.

The concept of redistributing the wealth comes from the egalitarian principle that poverty exists because one significant portion of society lacks the resources to advance its condition while the other portion does have access to these resources. Since the lagging portion of society lacks the resources to ameliorate its condition, it is believed that only the state can right the wrong. The state has, then, become the great equalizer to ensure that members of society have an equitable and fair access to scarce resources. Of course, we all want those who are materially disadvantaged, to have the same opportunities as those who already have access to resources. But the ideology that lies behind the motivation to redistribute the wealth is rooted in the belief that those who have access to resources, have access because they stole these resources from those who currently do not have access to it. To fix the issue, those who argue that everyone should have access to resources believe that the state is the only entity to redistribute these resources equally. However, there is a quintessential flaw within that approach to redistribute the wealth.

The state is fundamentally propertied-less. What it is said to be government-propertied is in fact taxpayer-propertied. That being said, in order for the state to enforce the redistribution of wealth, or to "equitably and fairly" redistribute the wealth, it can only give it to the have-nots by taking from the haves; which means, it must take the resources of those who have it and give it to those who do not have it. In other words, it is colloquially said: "The state can only give to Peter what it takes away from Paul." If the state was propertied on its own, it would not have to coercively take the resources of those who have it and give it to those who do not have it. It could have simply given its own resources to those who lack them. But since it [the state] has no resources of its own, it is compelled to forcibly take away the resources of those who have it and give it to those who do not have it. Now the great question here is to know if it is morally right to arbitrarily deprive someone of his property and resources and give it to someone else simply because that person does not have it? Since the need to redistribute the wealth comes from a moral argument, that redistributing the wealth is morally right according to egalitarians; then we can safely answer, however, that confiscating or arbitrarily depriving someone's property or resources and give it to the one who lacks; is not morally right. It is theft for the fact of the matter. Depriving someone arbitrarily of his property and resources or confiscating his assets without his consent is theft. Therefore, the redistribution of wealth by state-means is morally wrong. The redistribution of wealth in itself is not a bad concept at all. Redistributing the wealth simply means transferring income or wealth from some individuals to others by means of social mechanism. Charity is a perfect example of redistribution of wealth. J.K. Rowling, for example, willingly gave a portion of her assets to charity. She did it out of altruism, out of free-will, voluntarily and willingly. No one has coerced the bestselling author to forcibly and compulsorily give her money or assets to charity. She has decided willingly to do so. That kind of wealth redistribution is morally right. On the other hand, redistributing the wealth by state-means is not morally right. Forcing individuals to be altruistic is not the way to truly deliver altruistic results.

To redistribute the wealth "equitably," the state uses compulsory methods to achieve these goals. One of those compulsory methods is the progressive income tax. This taxation system overtaxes some individuals, precisely those who earn yearly a significant income that ensconces them within the top 20 percent of the wealthiest in society. The progressive income tax is based on the stipulation that those who earn more revenues should pay more in taxation, they should pay their "fair share." But the principal conundrum with the progressive income tax is that it is arbitrary and promulgates income inequality. The progressive income tax is, as a matter of fact, the reflection of a punishment. It punishes the haves; those who are wealthy and have access to resources. It punishes them for having access to resources. It punishes them for being wealthy. Despite its good intent at wanting to make things even or fairer, the progressive income tax does quite the opposite. Let's use a fictional example to illustrate how the progressive income tax is an unfair tax system that generates more inequality. Tom, who worked 20 hours a week, had a different work ethic from his brothers, Dick and Harry, who each worked 60 hours per week.[36] Neither Tom's nor Dick's wives worked, while Harry's wife worked 40 hours per week as an office manager making $50,000 per year.[37] Tom and Dick spent all of their income, and were relying on Social Security to take care of them when they retired.[38] Harry and his wife, on the other hand, saved most of their after-tax income over many years, gradually accumulating $300,000. They

---

[36] Hagopan, Kip, "The Inequity of the Progressive Income Tax." *Policy Review.* The Hoover Institution. (2011). https://www.hoover.org/research/inequity-progressive-income-tax. Article.

[37] Ibid.
[38] Ibid.

invested this money in bonds and real estate that produced $25,000 a year in interest and rental income.[39] Tom makes $25,000 per year, Dick's family makes $75,000 per year, and Harry and his wife both make $150,000 per year since they both work and jointly file their taxes.[40] Under a progressive income tax, Harry's family will be paying more than Dick and Tom although Harry has been working over 60 hours a week and his wife has been working over 40 hours a week. Harry and his wife have both saved their money cautiously so that they will get to spend it on relevant things such as real estate or other kind of assets that will be long-term beneficial to them. With the progressive income tax, Harry and his wife will be taxed over 30 percent of their income while Dick will be taxed around 20 percent and Tom will be taxed at less than 10 percent. The argument that progressive taxation increases worker productivity, yielding greater economic efficiency and higher

---

[39] Ibid.
[40] Ibid.

aggregate income[41] is fallacious. It is fallacious because the one who is less taxed will not be incentivized to work more because if the less-taxed person tried to work more and produces more, she will be taxed more. To avoid paying more taxes, people with lower incomes will attempt to maintain the income they have so that they will be less taxed. Consequently, income inequality enlarges itself because people in low-income brackets refuse to earn higher wages so they will get to pay lower taxes while those who earn higher wages are no less wealthy despite the application of the progressive tax system upon them.

The progressive income tax is only one factor of compulsory wealth redistribution. Another way in which compulsory wealth redistribution takes place is through the creation of a social safety net or more commonly known as the welfare state. The idea of creating a social safety net comes from, yet,

---

[41] Ibid.

again the moral argument for which the wealth should be redistributed equally. The have-nots shall have the same access to scarce resources as the haves have. And the purpose of the welfare state is to ensure that the have-nots do have access to these resources one way or another. Despite the good intentions of the welfare state, it has failed to deliver the results that the disenfranchised of our society were wholeheartedly expected. The welfare state has, in fact, created a system of cultural dependency that has deepened the impoverishment of lagging communities. If we take a close look at the African American community for example, before the promulgation of the welfare state in the United States, in 1960 just 22 percent of black children were raised in single-parent families.[42] In the early 2010, more than 70 percent of black children were raised

---

[42] Williams, Walter E., *The Welfare State's Legacy*. Creators. (2017). https://www.creators.com/read/walter-williams/09/17/the-welfare-states-legacy. Article. Web.

in single-parent families.[43] How come has the rate of children being raised in the single-parent household more than tripled within the last fifty years since the implementation of the welfare state? The policies of the welfare are the cause of this detrimental surge in the black community. A woman would receive higher welfare benefits if she had a child and not being married at the same time. This pernicious policy did not only emasculate black fathers, but it also created an environment where children would grow up fatherless. So, single black women were incentivized to not get married but to have babies while being unmarried if they wanted their "welfare income" to increase. This welfare policy has plunged a significant portion of the black community into the serfdom of poverty while other minority communities such as Asian and Indians are economically thriving. The welfare state has simply stimulated those who lack resources to not

---

[43] Ibid.

thoroughly have access to them. When the state heavily taxes the haves and collect these taxes to give it to the have-nots, it actually does not help the have-nots to emancipate themselves and join the haves. On the contrary, it creates a sense of entitlement for the have-nots who believe that they do not need to produce in order to receive the benefits of society's production. So, they are not encouraged to leave the state of poverty in which they are in because if they do, they will lose the benefits that they are earning without having to work. The welfare state is one of the major engines that amplifies the stratification of social class and income inequality. The bigger the welfare state becomes, the greater the stratification between the haves and the have-nots becomes, and the wider the wealth gap between people individuals becomes.

Income inequality can be narrowed if most people do work. If most people do work, it means that the state is less involved in economic affairs, which empowers individuals to have access to more opportunities and resources. Until then, the welfare state will remain that perpetual predicament that will continue to enslave, despite itself, the have-nots to be maintained in a state of poverty.

6.

Political Leaders and the Art of Resenting

There are many reasons for which income inequality exists and persists. One of the reasons enumerated was the fallacious assumption that one group of people takes resources away from others. This kind of conceptual method is called exploitation. Egalitarians have always argued that the social stratification in America is due to the fact that the rich have access to resources while the poor do not. And that the rich took away these resources for themselves from those who actually produce these resources; which means the poor. This is the Marxian message that has been conveyed in the collective consciousness since the nineteenth century. Since then it is widely believed that the have-nots have few to no resources because the haves have taken it away from them, and such attitude and concept justifies the aggrandizement of income inequality in America. The concept of social exploitation is only one factor in the blame for the widening of the social stratification. Discrimination and the lack of cultural receptivity are two essential factors that play a significant role in the enlargement income inequality.

One is fallacious and the other is valid. Saying that discrimination is the reason why some social groups are more advanced than others is preponderantly misleading. But the lack of cultural receptivity is, however, valid. It is undeniably true that some social groups are more economically advanced than other social groups. We know that the Black and Hispanic communities are the major lagging communities in the United States. But the Native American community is even more economically retrenched and isolated than the Black and Hispanic communities. Most members of the Native American community do live in reserved lands in the middle of the country while most communities have spread throughout the nation in various towns and cities. When we speak of discrimination in America, we usually refer to the concept that the white European population, which is the majority; is discriminating against minority social groups which encapsulate Asians, Arabs, Blacks, Indians (from India), Native Americans, and Hispanics. Interestingly, although the Asian and Indian communities are considered to be minorities due to their small representative number in the national community; with the Asian community making 5.6 percent and the Indian community making 1.3 percent of the national population according to the 2017 data of United States Census Bureau;[44] these two communities alone are substantially more economically advanced than the

---

[44] *Asian Alone or in Any Combination by selected Groups 2017.* U.S. Census Bureau (2017).

majority of white European Americans. It does not mean that every single American person of Asian or Indian origin is richer than a white American. It simply means that when we look at the majority of them in each community, their output is significantly higher than white Americans of European descents. The majority of Indian and Asian Americans are highly educated. They mainly have advanced degrees in hard sciences fields but also in other disciplines. For example, famous legal scholar and constitutional law professor Akhil Amar is American of Indian origins. He is considered to be one of the most influential legal thinkers in American jurisprudence, and he is doing economically better than the majority of white Americans. Manjul Bhargava, who is also a professor of mathematics at Princeton University, is an American of Indian origins who is doing economically far better than most white Americans. Famous actors, Kal Penn and Priyanka Chopra, who are also Americans of Indian origins, are economically well above the majority of white Americans. Steven Chu, former U.S. Secretary of Energy under the Obama administration, Nobel Prize-winner in physics and professor of physics, is an American of Chinese origins who is economically well above the majority of white Americans. Elaine Chao, U.S. Secretary of Transportation, is an American citizen born in Taiwan, who is also doing economically very well. Francis Fukuyama, famous political scientist, is also an American of Japanese origins who is economically well above the majority of white Americans. Robert Tsai, professor of law at American University and award-winning author, is also an American citizen originally from Taiwan who is doing economically better than most white Americans. All these names mentioned are all members of the Asian and Indian communities respectively. If minorities are economically lagging because the majority has deprived them of having access to resources due to discriminatory policies, how come Americans of Asian and Indian origins, who are demographically undersized, are doing significantly better than most whites Americans? Simply because disparity does not mean discrimination. There is a clear economic disparity between the white community and the Asian and Indian communities. If discrimination was truly the real cause that precludes minorities from economically and socially advancing, then the Asian and the Indian communities would have been hindered by it. The Asian and Indian communities are not the only minority groups that are economically successful. Furthermore, some members of the Black community have shown that discrimination is not the main factor of economic disparity between social groups. While the Asian and Indian communities mainly capitalize on academic education to generate economic success, the members of the Black community who have become wealthy, have capitalized on entertainment, business, sports, and politics. For example, Jay-Z, famous rapper, is the first American rapper to become a billionaire. That alone shows how much Jay-Z is much above most white Americans. Oprah Winfrey, Michael Jordan, Lebron James, Will Smith, Barack Obama, and Robert Smith; are prominent examples of Black Americans who have become economically prosperous in the United States. It does not mean that discrimination does not exist. It does not mean that discrimination is a meaningless impediment of our social order. Seeing individuals from minority social groups who have been economically more prosperous than white Americans, demonstrates that discrimination is not the cause of income inequality or economic disparity. What causes economic disparity between social groups is the choices that each individual within those groups makes and the personal responsibility to which each individual is held accountable for his actions.

Unlike discrimination, cultural unreceptiveness is a real and valid factor for stimulating income inequality. But it stimulates income inequality for the wrong reasons. The social groups that are economically lagging, are lagging not because their members are inherently poor but because their political leaders are the real impediment who preclude their people from economically rising. Political leaders in social groups that are economically lagging are the real conundrum to the rise of their people because they preach a rhetoric that incentivizes resentment. The political leader of a lagging community has all the incentives to not let his community prosper. Because if he does so, he will, not only become irrelevant, but he will also lose his grip on power. The general rhetoric of political leaders in lagging communities consists of saying that members of advanced social groups are prosperous because they steal the jobs of those who are lagging. For example, during the 1960s, the Ugandan economy was one of the most freshly advanced economies of the East African region following the independence era. Indians, who were a minority group, settled in Uganda for business and commerce purposes. They created market venues that did previously not exist before their arrival in Uganda. Fairly, Indians living in Uganda were economically more prosperous than local Ugandans since they were the ones who principally developed the Ugandan economy.[45] In the early 1970s, however, Idi Amin Dada, a political leader and demagogue, rose to power to establish a dictatorship upon the Ugandan people from 1971 to 1979. Amin Dada gained popularity among the Ugandan people through his hateful and resentful rhetoric. He blamed the Indians and other minority groups, who were economically more advanced than the local Ugandans, to be the ones who steal the jobs that local Ugandans were supposed to have. He blamed advanced social groups for the poverty and woes of the local Ugandans. Once Amin Dada became the leader of Uganda, one of his major and

---

[45] Jones, Ben, *The Two Sides of Uganda.* The Guardian. (2009). https://www.theguardian.com/society/katineblog/2009/may/26/uganda-and-poverty. Article. Web.

first policies was to expel Indians and other minority groups who have been economically thriving, from Uganda. The expulsion of Indians from Uganda was the main factor that led to the collapse of the Ugandan economy. The Indian community in Uganda was the most productive community in the country. They developed the economy and increased the living standard of the general Ugandan population. Amin Dada made the greatest mistake to expel Indians from the country because he thought that confiscating their material wealth would seriously impede their economic advancement. What Amin Dada has forgotten though, was that the true wealth of man is not his material assets but human capital. Human capital is what enables the production of material assets. By expelling those who mainly contributed to the advancement of the Ugandan economy, Amin Dada set his own people for failure because the local Ugandan population did not learn from the Indians how to develop their own capital. Their refusal to learn from the Indians how to develop economic resources, and creating new markets, did greatly contribute to the stagnation of the Ugandan economy. Hostility to more productive minorities, who both increase the national standard of living and provide cultural examples and opportunities for members of the majority population to acquire the human capital of a more advanced culture, in order to become more productive and advance themselves, might seem to be irrational.[46] But it is quite rational, from the standpoint of the self-interest of leaders of lagging groups, to keep the groups they lead resentful of more advanced groups, and to blame those advanced groups for their own group's failure to share more fully in the economic benefits created by skills and knowledge that are not as prevalent in the lagging group's own culture.[47] Uganda is not the only place where

---

[46] Sowell, Thomas, "Cultural Diffusion" *Wealth Poverty and Politics*, (2016). Basic Books. New York, New York. ISBN: 978−0-465-09676-3. Book. Print. P. 130-131.
[47] Ibid. P. 131.

political leaders rise to power through the proliferation of resentful rhetoric. Adolf Hitler did the same in Germany in order to become the leader of his country, by blaming Jews as the source of all the woes of the Germans. Making the German people resentful toward the Jews, who were a productive minority group, facilitated his ascension to political power.

Preaching resentment to a group of people who already lack the skills and knowledge to enhance the development of their community is to set this group for economic and social failure. The problem with political leaders in lagging social groups is that they make their people believe that political power is the path to economic prosperity. In other words, holding political power would determine the path to economic prosperity. Yet this assumption is blatantly deceitful. Among the minority groups living in America, the Black community is the community that has the most people who hold political office whether it is at the local, state, or federal level. Despite that unequivocal accomplishment for a social group that has enormously suffered from slavery and the Jim Crow laws, Black cities ran by Black political leaders have a worse socioeconomic condition than cities ran by white politicians. For example, Newark, New Jersey is a city that has always been governed predominantly by black politicians. Notwithstanding, the housing market has been crumbling due to a lack of good management by the municipality of the city which has failed to implement the right policies to sustain the housing boom. In Newark, 29 percent of its residents live in poverty[48], and the Newark Housing Authority has lost about $6 million a year in federal funding for the last 12 years.[49] Moreover the data show that Blacks have the highest rate of poverty in Newark with 40

---

[48] Yi, Karen, *It Could cost $26M to fix this crumbling public housing, but is it worth it?* NJ.com. (2018). https://www.nj.com/essex/2018/01/years_of_neglect_city_confronts_reality_of_public.html. Article. Web.

[49] Ibid.

percent while the Hispanic community has a poverty rate of 27 percent; Whites have a poverty rate of 14 percent and Asians have poverty rate of less than 2 percent.[50] Interestingly, the incumbent Mayor of Newark; who is Black and who has been Mayor since 2014; Ras Baraka; earns a salary of $130, 721 per year according to the Office of the Mayor of Newark while the Black residents of the city of Newark encompass the highest poverty rate of the city. They live in deteriorated and crumbling public housing; they lack access to basic needs, and most of them make a salary of less than $60,000 a year compare to their white and Asian counterparts. Newark is not the only city ran by a black politician which has a worst economic condition for black people. The city of Compton, in California, is also ran by a black mayor. Compare to Newark, New Jersey; the poverty rate in Compton is less striking

---

[50] Data USA for Newark, NJ.
https://datausa.io/profile/geo/newark-nj/. Data.

108

but remains nonetheless alarming with 23 percent[51] while it is 29 percent in Newark. In Compton, Hispanics, who are also a lagging group in America, have the highest rate of poverty of over 40 percent, while whites have 24 percent, Blacks have 18 percent, and Asians have less than 1 percent.[52] The case of Compton shows that Black people are doing slightly better than those living in Newark, New Jersey although their economic condition is not necessarily great. The example of Newark though substantiated that having political power does not lead to economic salvation. Newark is a city that is predominantly populated by African Americans, with a Black mayor who makes three times more than what his own people are making while they have the highest rate of poverty in the city. In the early twentieth century, the Irish community, which

---

[51] Data USA for Compton, CA.
https://datausa.io/profile/geo/compton-ca. Data.

[52] Ibid.

was among the lagging communities of white Americans of European descents, followed the same pattern; they used to believe that holding political power will pave the way to economic prosperity. They held major political offices in various capacities and at all level of government; to the point that they even had their first U.S. President ever in 1960 (JFK). But John F. Kennedy being the first American of Irish descents elected President of the United States did not systematically ameliorate the living standard of the Irish; the Germans, British, and Jews were the most prosperous communities among white American of European descents.

The most prosperous and advanced social groups such as Asians, Indians, Germans, Scandinavians, British, and the Dutch; are economically more advanced than Blacks, Italians, Hispanics, and Irish because they never intertwined politics and economics. They never believed that economic salvation was determined by political power. Instead, they rather stayed out of politics because they understood that seeking political power would impede the advancement of their economic activities. Social groups that are economically lagging are resentful because their leaders have told their people that it is not their fault if they are in this pernicious situation, but the fault of those who do not look like them, who have a different set of cultural values than them. Political leaders in lagging social groups have absolutely no intention nor incentives to advance the socioeconomic condition of their community because if they truly do, they will be no longer be relevant to the public. The essence of politics is emotion. A political leader cannot hold power if he sells attainable goals to his people. What makes politicians relevant, likeable, and as authorities; is that they promise unattainable goals to their people. The bigger and unrealistic the goal becomes, the more the people become inclined to vote for the leader, and the greater the power of the leader expands. If a political leader tells his people that they should use their knowledge, talents, skills, intelligence, and judgement to develop human capital instead of waiting for a central authority to solve the problems that they themselves can solve; it means that, that leader has committed his own political suicide. Keeping lagging-social-groups resentful is preponderantly quintessential to achieve political power for any political leader from those groups. That is also why political leaders are the ones responsible for the enlargement of the inequality of income between social groups.

7.

The Middle-Class
and Taxation

The middle-class, in every civilized and advanced society, is the most significant social class in terms of economic mobility. The economy of a civilized society is built upon the middle-class, because that is where the majority of people produce the wealth of the society in which they live. What makes it different between the middle-class and the upper-class in the social hierarchy, is the amount of wealth, assets and resources accumulated in each social class. The upper-class has a greater accumulation of wealth than the middle-class because the majority of the people who are in the upper-class are owners of various assets while most middle-class people are not owners of multiple assets yet. For example, most middle-class people may be homeowners, but they pay a mortgage to retain the ownership of their home while upper-class people do not pay a mortgage because they either paid the house cash from the get-go, or they have already paid off their mortgage and now retain the full ownership of the house they own.

In the United States, the middle-class is the heart of the American economy. It is noteworthy to accentuate the middle-class is not a mere bloc of individuals within a social class. It is a social class divided mainly into two sub-classes, which are the lower-middle-class also known as the working-class, and the upper-middle-class also known as *la petite bourgeoisie* or to translate it English for "the small bourgeoisie." In the United States, the whole middle-class constitutes a slim majority of the American population, about 52 percent, but that is still less than it has been in nearly half a century.[53] The fundamental difference between the working-class and the small bourgeoisie lies in their difference of income. According to the 2018 Pew Research data, the aggregate median income of the whole middle-class is $78, 442 a year of as of 2016.[54] According to the U.S. Census Bureau, the household income of the working-class ranges between $20,000 and $44,999 while the household income for the small bourgeoisie ranges between $140,000 and $149,000.[55] The class between the two; the working-class and the small bourgeoisie; which is the middle

[53] Frankenfield, Jake, "Which Income Class Are You?" *Economics: Behavioral Economics.* Investopedia. (2019). https://www.investopedia.com/financial-edge/0912/which-income-class-are-you.aspx.

[54] Kochchar, Rakesh, "The American middle class is stable in size, but losing ground financially to upper-income families." *Pew Research Center.* (2018). https://www.pewresearch.org/fact-tank/2018/09/06/the-american-middle-class-is-stable-in-size-but-losing-ground-financially-to-upper-income-families/. Data.

[55] *2018 Household Income Survey,* U.S. Census Bureau. (2018). https://www.census.gov/data/tables/time-series/demo/income-poverty/cps-hinc/hinc-01.html. Data.

of the middle-class, makes between $45,000 and $139,999 a year. This class is constituted of working-class people and small bourgeois combined. It is the most flexible bracket because it ensures the migration of people between the working-class and the small bourgeoisie. The data of the U.S. Census is unequivocally accurate, nonetheless, it is important to comprehend that the middle-class as a social class is not a stagnant class where median incomes are motionless. A working-class person can be considered to be in the upper-class if she makes generally over $60,000 a year. There is no irrefutable data that determines that the set income to make in order to be considered a small bourgeois within the middle-class is $140,000 per year. That income will eventually increase as the middle-class keeps growing. Between 2020 and 2025, the median income household to be considered upper-middle-class may slightly or significantly augment, depends on the social mobility that is being effectuated within the middle-class; and it also depends on the purchasing power people have. The bigger the purchasing power is, the more people get to spend, the smaller the purchasing power is, the more people are compelled to save.

Taxation is one of the factors that determines the ability of the purchasing power of a person or a social class. The other factor is inflation, and it will be discussed in the next essay. The purchasing power is entrenched after tax-deductibles. As the middle-class is the largest social class in most civilized societies, it is the one that gets to pay more than everyone in taxation. Furthermore; with the sub-classes that encompass the middle-class, people are taxed differently within the middle-class, which ascertains the inequality of income within that social class. Income inequality has recently become an essentially political predicament because politicians use it as a weapon during electoral campaigns to secure votes. Many politicians, especially on the Left, have used it as a rhetorical issue to empower the state to redistribute the wealth "equitably," and tax everyone "fairly." As it was explained in the fifth essay, the progressive income tax is more of a conundrum on the middle-class and the upper-class because they get to pay more than any other social class. Every time a government program is created and implemented; this program is generated by the taxes collected from the social classes that contribute to the economy. The middle-class pays more in taxes than any other social class because it is the social class that makes a wide range of various income going from $45,000 all the way to $250,000 income and more. To be clear, all Americans are paying fewer federal taxes than they have in recent decades.[56] Tax cuts authored by President George W. Bush were maintained by President Obama before President Trump's 2017 Tax and Jobs Act further cut taxes.[57] Under Trump, the wealthiest 20

---

[56] Coleman, Patrick, A. *Middle Class Parents Need to Do the Math on Taxes.* Fatherly. (2019). https://www.fatherly.com/love-money/middle-class-parents-rethink-progressive-taxes/. Article. Web.

[57] Ibid.

percent who once had to pay estate tax on any wealth transfer of $5 million have seen that threshold increase to $11 million, which is a $6 million savings in the estate tax that will be invested and compounded.[58] The tax cuts policy of President Trump enhances the purchasing power of the taxpayer. The less taxes to pay, the greater the power to spend more is ensconced. State taxes are the taxes that truly affect the middle-class. Instead of enforcing a progressive income tax at the state level, a flat tax would be better because everyone would be truly paying their "fair share" at the same rate. A flat income tax is also doable at the federal level, but government needs to be significantly limited before such system could be effectively implemented.

---

[58] Ibid,

8.

Unemployment and Inflation

Unemployment is evidently a factor of every economy. It is evident that everyone is employable, but everyone cannot be employed at the same time. Everyone is employable because we are all human beings. As human beings, we possess the first wealth that enables us to create material wealth; which is human capital. As Professor Sowell has always described, human capital is what people have in their head; their brain, their ability to generate thoughts, to stimulate their intelligence, and to acquire knowledge. Human capital is the first resource to be used for any kind of task to be completed and for any kind of tangible resources to be produced. So, anyone is employable because every human being is a resource in itself.

But Every single human being is not and cannot be employable at the same time. The point here, is to understand why, if all human beings are an intrinsic resource in itself, then why everyone could not be employed in order to eradicate unemployment? All politicians, without exception, always promise to either reduce unemployment or to eradicate it completely. The less charismatic ones, on the one hand, try to remain realistic by promising to reduce unemployment, which means that some people will not be able to work but unemployment on aggregate on the general population will be substantially reduced. The most charismatic ones, on the other hand, promise to totally eradicate unemployment; which means that every single member of society will have a job regardless of what the economic situation is and regardless of how it evolves. Ideally, eradicating unemployment would be the perfect situation to skyrocket productivity. But eradicating unemployment is fundamentally utopian. It is utopian because the economic condition of a society is based on recessions and expansions. During times of economic expansion, more people are employed because there is productivity; there is more wealth to be created because inflation is low; so, the price of production is affordable, and people can spend more. During times of economic recession, many people lose their jobs because there is not enough money to pay the workers since inflation is higher, and the cost of labor becomes expensive.

One significant factor that creates unemployment, is not the lack of human capital, but the regulations that the state imposes upon the private sector to hire workers. In other words, the minimum wage law is an impediment that inflates unemployment rate in a given society. The philosophical purpose of the minimum wage is based upon a moral argument, which is to prevent an employer to pay a worker less than a given wage set by the state otherwise, the employer could abuse the labor of the worker without just compensation. The philosophical purpose of the minimum wage is rooted in *The Condition of the Working Class in England* (1844), book written by Marxist philosopher, Friedrich Engels, who described the horrendous conditions in which the workers were working, and argued that the absence of a minimum wage imposed by the state, enabled the capitalist bourgeois to exploit the labor of the workers and to pay them a wages below the level of subsistence. This premise is morally comprehensible, but the real effect of the minimum wage is the most significant factor that actually creates unemployment. It creates unemployment because it precludes the employer to hire low-skilled workers. Without the minimum wage, the employer gets to hire who he wants and pays the employee at whatever wage he wants. Employment is a form of contract. When a prospective employee accepts to work for a private entity, he subsequently enters into a contract with his employer. This contract is voluntary. It is voluntary because the employer, at the moment proposing a giving wage to the prospective employee, does so without any form of coercion. He only suggests to the prospective employee that the wage that he is proposing to pay him is, in his view, the wage that the prospective employee worth in terms of skills and value. The prospective employee has the right and choice to either accept or reject the proposal submitted to him by the employer. If he accepts; he, then, has to comply and abide by the rules and regulations of the employer. If he rejects the proposal, he has the freedom to seek employment elsewhere where the wage proposed to him could probably be better than the one that was previously proposed. The prospective employee is free to choose wherever he wants to work. However, if he is unsatisfied with the conditions under which he is working, he has the freedom to leave and seek employment elsewhere. Moreover, the worker is protected by the labor laws effectuated by the state, which prevent an employer to inflict harrowing working conditions upon a worker. It is important to fathom that the purpose of the minimum wage is not to make living wage, but simply to prevent an employee from being paid below the level of subsistence at an entry-level position. The minimum wage is only effective for an entry-level position; and not beyond. That being said, even if a low-skilled employee was paid at a very low wage, he is not condemned to earn that wage for the rest of his life. Without the minimum wage, the low-skilled individual has the opportunity to be employed in a place where he is not normally expected to be employed due to his lack of skills. Within the concept of social mobility, a low-skilled employee has the chance to climb the ladder by gaining professional experience, developing a new skillset, and moving along by acquiring a disciplinary attitude toward work. The majority of people who are paid by the minimum wage are mostly teenagers, college students, and recent college graduates; because those are the people who are low-skilled, they are the ones who enter the workforce once they have completed their studies or are apt to start working because they are full of energy and are able-bodied.

The minimum wage law, as a matter of fact, hurts those that it intended to help, which means the low-skilled workers. It hurts them the most because it inhibits employers to hire them due to their lack competence or limited skillset. The implementation of the minimum wage affects primarily small businesses because they are the ones that need low-skilled workers to complete the most elementary tasks. When the state increases the minimum wage, it also increases the cost of labor, which makes employers reluctant to hire a low-skilled worker and paying him at a wage higher than what his skills actually worth. For example, as the minimum wage became $14 an hour in Washington, D.C. as of July 2019, it will be ten times harder for young teenagers and low-skilled worker to work at places like Whole Foods or McDonalds because no employers would be willing to pay a low-skilled worker $14 an hour just to scan items or mob the floor if that same employer could buy machinery to perform the same tasks and at a lower cost. A study by Jeffrey Clemens and Michael Wither evaluated the effect of minimum wage increases on low-skilled workers during the recession and found that minimum wage between December 2006 and December 2012, it reduced the national employment-population ratio by 0.7 percent points.[59] That amounts to about 1.4 million jobs. And more noteworthy; that, binding minimum wage increases significantly reduced the likelihood that low-skilled workers rose to what we characterize as lower middle-class earnings.[60] And while the large majority of those pushing for an increase in the minimum wage have good intention, this has certainly not always been the case; much like rent controls, increasing the minimum wage reduces the price of discrimination by creating a surplus of

---

[59] Syrios, Andrew, *Yes, Minimum Wages Still Increase Unemployment.* Mises Institute. (2015). https://mises.org/library/yes-minimum-wages-still-increase-unemployment. Article. Web.

[60] Ibid.

laborers for employers to choose from.[61] Increasing the minimum wage creates unemployment and enlarges the wealth gap. Furthermore, it simply paves the way for employers to easily discriminate against low-skilled workers and minorities as well. For example, according to an analytical study conducted by Professor Thomas Sowell, in 1948, the unemployment rate among black 16-year-olds and 17-years-olds was 9.4 percent, slightly lower than that of white kids of the same ages, which was 10.2 percent. Over the decades since then, we have gotten used to unemployment rates among black teenagers being over 30 percent, 40 percent or in some years even 50 percent.[62]

The more the state increases the minimum wage, the more unemployment also increases. But the augmentation of the minimum wage is based on inflation. The higher inflation is, the higher the minimum wage will be increased as well, because

---

[61] Ibid.
[62] Ibid.

the whole economic purpose of creating the minimum wage in the first place, was to keep up with inflation since inflation is the main factor that determines the purchasing power of the consumer. When politicians like Bernie Sanders, Kirsten Gillibrand, or Elizabeth Warren argue that the minimum wage should be increased to $15-an-hour to make it a living wage, they quintessentially ignore that the living wage is not based on the minimum but it is based on the market value and the market value is determined by the rate of inflation. The market value is higher when the inflation is higher. The price of goods and services, property tax, and rent price increase as the rate of inflation surges. As the rate of inflation surges, the purchasing power of consumer becomes constrained. His [the consumer] ability to spend becomes limited, interest rates are higher, so the power to borrow is also reduced. As the minimum wage became $14-an-hour in Washington, D.C., it suggests that the price of goods and services, the price of property and rent have also raised, which means that the purchasing power of the low-skilled workers living in D.C. is more constrained than ever. They have a hard time affording buying a property if what they make is considered to be within the poverty threshold in Washington. People with more work experience have nothing to fear about the raise of the minimum wage because their salary is not based on the minimum wage. It is only for low-skilled workers that the minimum wage is a serious predicament. However, although the minimum wage does not affect skilled workers, it nonetheless affects the rate of unemployment and the economy as a whole. As long as inflation increases, bureaucrats will concurrently increase the minimum wage; but this increase will hurt low-skilled workers and employers who are seeking new workers to enhance their productivity. Furthermore, the minimum wage affects low-skilled workers, especially those who live in unsafe neighborhoods because in such neighborhoods, the poverty rate is substantially high since young teenagers are not hirable because the wage is above their skillset. These young people are either compelled to sign up for welfare in order to survive or find a way to leave the neighborhood and migrate toward another area where the living standard is better with more productivity.

Truth be told, unemployment is a perpetual factor of any economy within any given society. Eradicating unemployment is quasi-impossible despite the well-intended motivation because every individual, despite being a resource in itself, cannot be employable everywhere and in every market venue. The best way to reduce unemployment to the smallest scope possible is to incentivize more competition in the private sector, more deregulations in the labor laws so that low-skilled workers have also a chance to become an asset on the job market, to climb the ladder, and to move to the middle-class.

9.

Personal Behavior and Incentives

It is evidently clear that all human beings do not have the same social status. As it was ascertained in the previous essays, human beings were not born under same socioeconomic conditions. Some were born rich, other poor; some were born tall, others short, some were born healthy, and others were born with health predicaments, some were born able-bodied, others were born with some physical or mental disabilities. That being said, we are all inherently unequal. Human beings do not choose their socioeconomic condition, their health condition, nor their cultural upbringing at birth. There is nothing predestined that set forth the professional career in which an individual will embark on regardless of his socioeconomic condition. For example, President Nixon was a man who came from a very modest family where most of his relatives had a limited education. When Nixon was born in 1913, nothing predestined him that he would become the 37th President of the United States. His father was a grocer, and his mother, that he used to call a "saint," was a housewife. Both of his parents were no attorneys, no doctors, no professors, no venture capitalists, or famous artists. They were simple Quakers who did not have an extended education to advance their personal careers. Richard Nixon made the conscious decision to embark himself into a political career and he was determined, by all means, to become one day President of the United States. As it was aforementioned, no one gets to choose his socioeconomic condition, but it is our responsibility to change our socioeconomic condition if we were born in characteristically arduous and laborious conditions. This means that personal behavior and incentives are a fundamental factor within the ascension of the social hierarchy.

As income inequality exists in every civilized nation, whether it is a developed nation, a developing nation, or an underdeveloped nation; it is, at least fair to say that, if some people have a better income than others, it is partially because of the choices they have made which have led them to where they are today. The logical Marxian fallacy, which argues that the wealthy are wealthy because they have taken the resources they have from the poor, is fundamentally erroneous. Egalitarians who support that fallacious premise, fail to take personal responsibility into account as a crucial and critical factor in the creation of wealth. Let's not forget that every human being is by nature a resource, because we all possess a human brain, which is the organ that gives us the ability to think, to absorb information, to acquire knowledge, and to use that knowledge to develop scarce resources. The brain is the very first resource that a human being possesses. As we possess a human brain, we, therefore, have the ability to make rational choices and decisions. If the exploitation of the rich over the poor is specious belief, what concretely creates income inequality between people? The answer is personal behavior, choices, decisions, and responsibility.

Professor of Economics Walter E. Williams used to famously asseverated that there are five fundamental principles to follow in order to avoid long-term poverty and to ensure that oneself is climbing the ladder, elevating oneself from one social class to another. The first principle is to graduate high school. Indeed, an individual who has earned a high school degree is already a competitive asset in the labor market, especially for menial jobs such as becoming a carpenter, a plumber, a cosmetologist, a barber, an electrician, and for administrative jobs such as an administrative assistant or for entrepreneurial jobs such as a salesman and entrepreneurship. Earning a high school diploma is an access that ensures economic and social mobility for those who are not interested in pursuing a higher education. According to the Bureau of Labor Statistics, the median weekly earnings of a high school graduate in 2017 was about $700 a week.[63] The second principle is to not be having a child without being married in one's youth. When a teenager or young adult in his early twenties is a parent without being married, it precludes that young individual, who is now a parent, to aim for better career opportunities that could thoroughly advance one's professional life. According to a 2015-study published in the *Journal of Adolescent Health*, 16.8 percent of teenagers had been pregnant at least once at age 17.[64] When two young adults, without any high school degree, or without any sort of

[63] *Measuring the Value of Education*. Bureau of Labor Statistics. (2017). https://www.bls.gov/careeroutlook/2018/data-on-display/education-pays.htm. Data.

[64] Sarah K Garwood, MD, Gerassi Lara, PhD, Jonson-Reid Melissa, PhD, Plax Katie, MD, and Drake Brett, PhD. "More Than Poverty— Teen Pregnancy Risk and Reports of Child Abuse Reports and Neglect" *The Journal of Adolescent Health*. (2015); Volume 57(2): 164-168. DOI:10.1016/jadohealth.2015.05.004. Article.

professional skills, make the decision to have a child while they are not married and remain relatively immature within that age range, they are doomed to work several low-skilled jobs that pay very little, which make it even harder to support the welfare of the child. Having a child at 16, 17 or even 18 years of age is a poor choice that one who has made that choice, is condemned to live with it. It does not mean either that having a child at 23 years of age and unmarried is a better condition. Most 23-years-olds are recent college graduates who are looking for employment on the labor market. Teenage pregnancy sets young adults for failures and sentences them in the bottom 20 percent of the social hierarchy. It does not mean, however, that a young teen who has a child and unmarried, will never ever succeed; he or she may succeed, but his or her wrong decision to have that child at such an early age is a serious predicament to his or her own socioeconomic advancement. The unmarried-teenage parent will be required by the state to pay for child support; so, most of his or her paycheck will be tax-deducted by the state to ensure that the welfare of the child is being subsidized. The third principle is to be married before having children. A young couple that is married and has conceived during the marriage, has a stronger likelihood to move along the social mobility and to elevate themselves in the social hierarchy, principally for two reasons. The first reason is based upon the fact that, if the husband and the wife are both working, they have a stronger and higher income because their taxes are filed jointly. Both of their revenues are counted as one, which facilitate their ability to support their child or children's welfare. The second reason is that, even if the young father is the only one who works, and his wife is a housewife taking care of the child at home, the young father will have a higher income because he has two other individuals to feed. But since he is married, it shows that he is a responsible person who fully takes responsibility for his whole family. It is an incentive to move forward from one social class to a better one. For example, a 2005 study at Ohio University found that after getting married, people saw a sharp increase in their level of wealth.[65] After ten years of marriage, the couples reported an average net worth of around $43,000 compared to $11,000 for people who had stayed single.[66] The fourth principle to avoid long-term poverty is to take whatever job available to oneself. Indeed, no one likes cleaning floors, doing dishes for several hours on a daily basis, delivering mails all day at different locations within the neighborhood, or flipping burgers on a regular basis at a fast-food restaurant. But this is the kind of jobs that do not require any specific kind of training or skillset; anyone can perform these jobs. Despite the fact that these odd jobs are generally futureless, and without a concrete career prospect; they nonetheless

---

[65] Livingstone, Amy, *Financial Benefits of Marriage vs. Being Single – What's Better?* Money Crashers. https://www.moneycrashers.com/financial-benefits-marriage-single/. Article.

[66] Ibid.

offer to the low-skilled individual, an opportunity to gain some professional experience, to build a credit score which will enable him to take loans and to buy properties, and more importantly, it forces the low-skilled individual to be disciplined in the work environment. Odd jobs are not meant to make a career out of it. They are short-termed jobs. They are simply meant to give an opportunity to the low-skilled person to compete with others who are already established in the professional environment. Since odd jobs are short-termed jobs, they give incentives to low-skilled people to aim higher, to seek better opportunities to advance their socioeconomic condition. The fifth and last principle to avoid long-term poverty, is to avoid having a criminal record. It is conspicuously clear that employers are significantly reluctant to hire an individual with a criminal record. In fact, in most cases, having a criminal record automatically disqualifies the job applicant who has it. Having a criminal record makes of oneself a liability to the employer and to the company. An individual who has a criminal record in his adolescence and in his young adulthood, will have a hard time escaping the state of poverty. His likelihood to find employment is substantially limited, he will generally have a very low credit score because he cannot work, consequently he cannot be eligible to rent property or to take any kind of loan. A 2018 study conducted by Brookings Institute shows that one-third of men age 30 without any earnings are either incarcerated or unemployed former prisoners.[67] Of the 17 percent of men age 30 that have no earnings in 2012, about 3.5 percent were in prison or jail and another 3 percent are former prisoners without work— combined, they make up more than a third of all non-working men age 30.[68] Therefore, having a

---

[67] Looney, Adam, *5 facts about prisoners and work, before and after incarceration.* Brookings Institute. (2018). https://www.brookings.edu/blog/up-front/2018/03/14/5-facts-about-prisoners-and-work-before-and-after-incarceration/. Article. Web.

[68] Ibid.

criminal record greatly impedes one's ability to be financially independent and to climb the social ladder.

These five principles elaborated, encapsulate the notion of responsibility, choices, and decisions, as the quintessential factor to avoid long-term poverty. The life we each live is grounded on the concept of cause-and-effect. Regardless of the decisions we make on a daily basis; each decision we make affects us and our surroundings directly and indirectly, whether it is on a short-term or long-term basis. Good and wise decisions lead to positive consequences. Bad and foolish decisions lead to adversarial and predicamental consequences. Successful and wealthy people are not hazardously wealthy. They have made decisions that have led them to the results they sought. For example, a man that comes from a very poor family, but has decided to pursue an education; does his homework and manages to graduate high school, then even goes on to college and gets his bachelor's degree; has a strong likelihood to become successful and economically stable despite his laborious socioeconomic background compared to a person who has the same laborious background, but chose instead to do drugs, and to have a child while being unemployed. The consequence is relatively self-evident for these two examples. The one who chose to pursue his education, and makes rational choices to advance his condition, gives himself the opportunity and the ability to escape the state of poverty while the one who chose to do drugs and to have a child at a stage of his/her life where things are not quite into place; is making his or her own life more difficult than it already is, which means they are setting themselves to fail; they are propelling themselves into a long-term state of poverty. Rational choices and behavior develop higher incentives to do better, to seek bigger, and to achieve greater; while poor and irrational choices disincentivize people to be independent, and responsible. Poor decisions subvert the sovereignty of the individual. Because regardless of the kind of decisions we make, we have to face the consequences of those decisions. Rational choices provide opportunities in difficult times while irrational choices preclude opportunities from arising during difficult times. What we end up becoming or achieving in life is based upon the decisions we have made throughout the course of our aggregated actions.

146

10.

Political Decisions and Economic Outcomes

Political decisions have a serious impact on economic outcomes when the state attempts to intervene; to regulate economic activities. Government intervention has, overall, done more harm than good in attempting to narrow the income inequality gap. Government intervention in the economy and in social affairs, is a consequential impediment on economic activities for two essential reasons. The first reason is that, the state endeavors to control prices of production in the market. The second reason is that, once the state controls prices of production; it gets to dictate what the outcomes should be. In trying to control the market's production's prices, the state enforces a system of price that is ensconced below the market price. The predicament with ensconcing a price system below the market price, is that it creates a shortage of supply of the production being regulated. For example, let's say hypothetically that the state has taken control over the milk industry. Before the state intervenes in that industry and takes control over the means of production, the price of milk was set at $4.99 a gallon. That is the price that all the enterprises and factories that produced milk, agreed upon to compete. Based on demand, the price of milk fluctuates. When demand is high, the producers of milk increase the price by 2 percent so that the rate of demand would equalize the rate of supply. When demand is low, the producers of milk reduce the price of milk so that it will stimulate more people to buy milk so that more milk could be produced. The producers of milk know how to redistribute their product, they allocate it according to how much they can afford, and how much they can afford is based on how much they can produce. Then, the state steps in, and decides to take of control of the price system. It imposes a price below that of the market. As milk cost $4.99 a gallon under the market, the state reduces the price to $2.50 a gallon. As the price was significantly diminished, more people can afford to buy milk. As more people can afford to buy milk, the rate of demand for milk increased exponentially. As demand keeps increasing, there is, then, less milk to supply to everyone who wants it because the state did not produce enough milk for everyone. As the state failed to supply milk to everyone, that failure created a shortage of supply. The question is why did the state fail to produce enough milk for everyone? Simply because the state lacked some information that were crucial to the production of milk. If a gallon of milk cost $4.99, it is because the producers of milk knew that within that price, there is the cost of production which encapsulates manufacturing the milk, producing the box that would contain the milk, and the cost of transportation that would carried the milk from the factories to the stores. The state failed to take these factors into account before dropping the price below its nominal value. Price are signals that the parties in the transaction agreed upon to convey their exchange. As the state mingles in that transaction, it subsequently subverts the arrangements made between the two parties, and the results is most likely a failure.

Bureaucrats; despite the advanced degrees that they have earned from the best academic institutions in the society they live in, which epitomize that they are greatly qualified and highly skilled to make adequate judgment and rational decisions to conduct civil policy; still do not possess all the knowledge and possible information to determine the outcome of economic activities despite the abundance of resources available to them. The reason why bureaucrats, politicians and government officials, fail to rightly determine economic outcomes is because they wrongly attempt to measure opportunity by outcome. Measuring opportunity by outcome suggests that, based on what the outcome will be or is supposed to be, opportunities are accordingly allocated to match that outcome. The problem with that method is that, it seeks to control factors that are not controllable by human ability. The Soviet economy is a perfect example of that method. The Soviet government was an organization of highly intelligent and skilled individuals whom have all the knowledge possible to run an economy. They, nonetheless, failed and the Soviet Union collapsed because despite the technological assets available to them to run the economy, over the two-third of the Russian population was living in severe poverty while a selected few were living like kings. Those selected few were the members of the Politburo; the bureaucrats that ran the Soviet state. The bureaucrats, despite their skills, failed the Soviet economy because they conveyed the economic activities of the state by measuring opportunities by outcome. They lacked the knowledge and information necessary to stimulate a flourishing economy because these informations that they lacked were only available in the marketplace. Since the Soviet economy was not a market economy, there was no valuable information available to those who controlled the economic activities of the Soviet Union. The materials they used to produce and conduct their economic activities had no value. They could not be exchanged and could not be reused because it had no price. The aggregated output of their production was significantly lower than the input they needed to conduct their economic activities. Consequently, the outcome of the Soviet economy was a disaster then a collapse. Based on what the outcome was designed to be, the Soviet government has attempted to allocated opportunities accordingly to the outcome they sought. It means that they quantified their outcome rather than quantifying their opportunities. If it has done the opposite, the Soviet economy would have prevailed.

Measuring opportunity by outcome provides long-term adversarial outcomes because it discriminates against some opportunities that could lead to a better result than the actual outcome being sought. But because some opportunities do not fit, or do not align with the result being sought, these opportunities are consequently dismissed although they could be valuable to our pursuit. And that is the problem with planification and that is why planned economies are doomed to fail in the long run. For example, affirmative action and public housing are good illustration of how measuring opportunity by outcome delivers predicamental outcomes. With affirmative action, for example, schools focus on having a certain number of students that would fit certain criteria. Based on these criteria, the school sets quotas in which those students shall fit. This part reflects the outcome. The school, then, will impose a set of requirements that prospective students shall meet if they want to be admitted in the school. If they do not meet these criteria, they cannot be admitted in the school. So, the school starts to discriminate against students who do not meet the criteria they are seeking for. By discriminating against those students who do not meet the criteria they seek, they are dismissing students that could bring a substantial value to their program. That part reflects the opportunities being allocated according to the outcome being sought. Let's fully illustrate this mechanism with a concrete, nonetheless, fictitious example. Let's say the law school of University Z seeks to admit 50 students in its program for this full calendar. The outcome that the law school seeks is to have over two-third of its student body to be constituted of students of minority groups, preferably blacks. The outcome is that the law school aims to reach is to have a student body of predominantly black students for the sake of diversifying the student body and giving a chance to low-income people to have a legal education. Since the goal is to have a student body that is predominantly black, the administrators of the law school, then, enforce their admission requirements by discriminating against students who are not principally black-skinned. By reducing opportunities for non-black-skinned students to attend their law school, the administrators are arbitrarily excluding these non-black-skinned students regardless of their academic credentials. Among the black students that the law school seeks to have in its program, the administrators will, here again, discriminate against some black students over others. They will put more emphasis on black students from low-income class than black students from higher-income class. Here too, black students from higher-income classes are being discriminated against lower-income black students. The administrators will accept only few high-income black students and a majority of low-income black students in the law school. Non-black-skinned students (Whites, Asians, and Hispanics) applying to that law school will be allocated within the remaining one-third of the student body. The point is, since the outcome was to have more black students than any other racial group in their student body; the administrators of the law school quantified those students, putting them into quotas, and dismissing those who do not fit the criteria necessary to obtain admission. To ensure that the law school has more low-income black students in its student body, the school will subsequently reduce its academic standards so that the low-income black students could gain admission while the other students who may have better academic credentials than the low-income black students, will nonetheless be dismissed because they do not fit the criteria that the law school has set to reach its goal. The exact same process is set forth for public housing, but this time, with social class and income as decisive factors rather than race. And that is the way and the reason why planned economies failed. They failed because they are regulating economic activities based on a set of criteria that the state sets forth to conduct its activities rather than let it play out on its own.

The reason why it is better to measure outcome by opportunity is because, since no one knows what the outcome will be, we capitalize on the opportunity available to us and see what outcome it could deliver. Opportunities are hypotheses, they are measurable and can be tested to verify their validity. If an opportunity is tested, and does not deliver the result expected, it can be modified and adjusted so that it falls into the outcome's scope being sought. On the other hand, outcomes could be also tested, but unlike opportunities, they cannot be modified nor adjusted. If the outcome tested does not deliver the result expected, there is no alternative to modify or adjust that result. Planned economies are grounded upon political decisions. When the state enforces laws on public housing, implements positive discriminatory laws in school or at the workplace, bureaucrats do not do so with the intent to necessarily even up everything. They are pursuing an institutional agenda, and the policies implemented must corroborate with the agenda being pursued by the bureaucrats. The decisions made by politicians and bureaucrats upon economic activities are fundamentally political before anything else. Bureaucrats, in making decisions from a political angle rather than from an economic or social angle on economic and social activities, impede those that these decisions were supposed to help. If we take the public housing case, for example, the decision to create public housing for people in the low-income bracket is a political decision that economically affects those it was meant to help. Those who live in state-subsidized housing are surely paying a low fee to live in it, but on the other hand, they are living in degraded conditions. As they are living in degraded conditions but at a lower cost, they are more inclined to vote for politicians who would promote more government and bureaucracy to solve economic and social problems over politicians who would advocate for more market and more privatization. Notwithstanding, those living in public housing have much difficulties to leave the state of poverty because they become accommodated to the conditions in which they live in. They become, consequently, disincentivized to move into a better neighborhood because the price of housing there is much higher and unaffordable for them, so they rather stay in an area where housing is affordable according to their purchasing power.

Political decisions play an enormous role in economic outcomes. It does because we, now, live in a regulated market economy where the state has a strong impact on how economic activities should be conducted and conveyed. If bureaucrats could make decisions according to the welfare of the people in need, income inequality could be substantially reduced. But making decisions in such direction will impede the bureaucrats' agenda. The institutional agenda of the bureaucrats is the core element of the policies they effectuate.

About the Author

Germinal G. Van is an author, essayist, libertarian writer, and philosopher. He has published several books including *The Problem Of Egalitarianism*. He has published several articles with the Libertarian Institute and the Foundation for Economic Education.

Mr. Van holds a bachelor's degree in political science from the Catholic University of America and a master's degree in political management from the George Washington University. He works as a political advisor for Joshua Flynn, political candidate running for the Illinois State legislature for the District 78.

Acknowledgements

Writing a book is always a great task to accomplish with a process that is usually never easy. During the process of writing this book, several people have dearly contributed in different ways to ensure that this manuscript will come to life. My wife Elise has played a significant role in the accomplishment of this manuscript. She brought the support I need to complete the writing.

Secondly; I would like to thank Joshua Flynn, political candidate for the Illinois State Legislature for the District 78; for his diligent contribution to the completion of this manuscript.

REFERENCES

1. Coverage under the FLSA. The Fair Labor Standard Act. Department of Labor. https://www.flsa.com/coverage.html.

2. Ibid.

3. Ibid.

4. Editors, *How Much Money Do The Top Income Earners Make?* Financial Samurai. https://www.financialsamurai.com/how-much-money-do-the-top-income-earners-make-percent/. Article. Web.

5. Seiler, Edward; Jenkins, John H. "Isaac Asimov FAQ," *Isaac Asimov Home Page.* (June 27, 2008).

6. Editors, "Equality of Outcome," *Equality of Opportunity and Education. McCoy Family Center for Ethics in Society.* Stanford University.

7. Mason, Andy, "Equal Opportunity," *Encyclopedia Britannica.* Article History.

8. Huff, Richard, "Human Capital," *Encyclopedia Britannica*, Article. History.

9. Ibid.

10. OECD (2019), Real GDP forecast. doi: 10.1787/1f84150b-en (Accessed on 07 August 2019).

11. "Niger GDP Annual Growth Rate." *Trading Economics.* https://tradingeconomics.com/niger/gdp-growth-annual

12. Glenn-Marie Lange, Quentin Wodon, and Kevin Carey. *The Changing Wealth of Nations 2018.* World Bank Group. ISBN: 978-1-4648-1046-6. Book.

13. Ngcamu, Johannes Peter, *The History and Development of Black Entrepreneurship in South Africa.* Faculty of Economic and Management Science at Rand Afrikaans University. (2002). https://core.ac.uk/download/pdf/18219248.pdf. Dissertation.

14. Moses, Bernard, "The Economic Condition of Spain in the Sixteenth Century." *Journal of Political Economy*. Vol. 1; No 4. (Sep. 1893) pp.513-534. Published by the University of Chicago. Article.

15. Ibid.

16. Paralegal and Legal Assistants, *Occupational Outlook Handbook*. Bureau of Labor Statistics. https://www.bls.gov/ooh/legal/paralegals-and-legal-assistants.htm. Data.

17. Professors, Ibid.

18. Sowell, Thomas, *Economic Mobility*. Creators. (2013). https://www.creators.com/read/thomas-sowell/03/13/economic-mobility. Article.

19. Ibid.

20. Ibid.

21. Helm, Angela, *African Are the Most Educated Immigrants in US: Report*. The Root. (2018) https://www.theroot.com/africans-are-the-most-educated-immigrants-in-u-s-repo-1822169956. Article. Web.

22. Ibid.

23. Ibid.

24. Crossman, Ashley, *What Is Social Mobility?* ThoughtCo.(2019). https://www.thoughtco.com/social-mobility-3026591. Article. Web.

25. Ibid.

26. Ibid.

27. Chappelow, Jim, "Keynesian Economics," *Investopedia*. (2019).

28. Worstall, Tim, *If you're a Keynesian Then You Must Believe the Minimum Wage Increases Unemployment*. Forbes.(2015). https://www.forbes.com/sites/timworstall/2015/06/13/if-youre-a-keynesian-then-you-must-believe-the-minimum-wage-increases-unemployment/#29024b1cea3d. Article. Web.

29. Amadeo, Kimberly, *Seven Causes of Unemployment*, The Balance. (2019). https://www.thebalance.com/causes-of-unemployment-7-main-reasons-3305596. Article. Web.

30. Moore, Stephen, *The Enduring Myth of FDR and the New Deal*. The Heritage Foundation. (2014). https://www.heritage.org/budget-and-spending/commentary/the-enduring-myth-fdr-and-the-new-deal. Article. Web.

31. Ibid.

32. Amadeo, Kimberly, *2001 Recession, Its Causes, Impact, and What Ended it*. The Balance. (2019).

https://www.thebalance.com/2001-recession-causes-lengths-stats-4147962. Article. Web.

33. Bureau of Labor Statistics (BLS) On Unemployment from 2009 to 2019. https://data.bls.gov/timeseries/LNS14000000?fbclid=IwAR10s52T5Z0JiM2ZqgCrGmL7fbcAIqp17QVtCZWjPlFRD0svU_riUm4d2cc

34. Ibid.

35. Ibid.

36. Hagopan, Kip, "The Inequity of the Progressive Income Tax." *Policy Review.* The Hoover Institution. (2011). https://www.hoover.org/research/inequity-progressive-income-tax. Article.

37. Ibid.

38. Ibid.

39. Ibid.

40. Ibid.

41. Ibid.

42. Williams, Walter E., *The Welfare State's Legacy.* Creators. (2017).

https://www.creators.com/read/walter-williams/09/17/the-welfare-states-legacy.
Article. Web.

43. Ibid.

44. *Asian Alone or in Any Combination by selected Groups 2017.* U.S. Census Bureau (2017).

45. Jones, Ben, *The Two Sides of Uganda.* The Guardian. (2009).
https://www.theguardian.com/society/katineblog/2009/may/26/uganda-and-poverty. Article. Web.

46. Sowell, Thomas, "Cultural Diffusion" *Wealth Poverty and Politics,* (2016). Basic Books. New York, New York. ISBN: 978–0-465-09676-3. Book. Print. P. 130-131.

47. Ibid. P. 131.

48. Yi, Karen, *It Could cost $26M to fix this crumbling public housing, but is it worth it?* NJ.com. (2018).
https://www.nj.com/essex/2018/01/years_of_neglect_city_confronts_reality_of_public.html. Article. Web.

49. Ibid.

50. Data USA for Newark, NJ. https://datausa.io/profile/geo/newark-nj/. Data.

51. Data USA for Compton, CA. https://datausa.io/profile/geo/compton-ca. Data.

52. Ibid.

53. Frankenfield, Jake, "Which Income Class Are You?" *Economics: Behavioral Economics.* Investopedia. (2019). https://www.investopedia.com/financial-edge/0912/which-income-class-are-you.aspx.

54. Kochchar, Rakesh, "The American middle class is stable in size, but losing ground financially to upper-income families." *Pew Research Center.* (2018). https://www.pewresearch.org/fact-tank/2018/09/06/the-american-middle-class-is-stable-in-size-but-losing-ground-financially-to-upper-income-families/. Data.

55. *2018 Household Income Survey*, U.S. Census Bureau. (2018). https://www.census.gov/data/tables/time-series/demo/income-poverty/cps-hinc/hinc-01.html. Data.

56. Coleman, Patrick, A. *Middle Class Parents Need to Do the Math on Taxes.* Fatherly. (2019). https://www.fatherly.com/love-money/middle-class-parents-rethink-progressive-taxes/. Article. Web.

57. Ibid.

58. Ibid,

59. Syrios, Andrew, *Yes, Minimum Wages Still Increase Unemployment.* Mises Institute. (2015). https://mises.org/library/yes-minimum-wages-still-increase-unemployment. Article. Web.

60. Ibid.

61. Ibid.

62. Ibid.

63. *Measuring the Value of Education.* Bureau of Labor Statistics.(2017). https://www.bls.gov/careeroutlook/2018/data-on-display/education-pays.htm. Data.

64. Sarah K Garwood, MD, Gerassi Lara, PhD, Jonson-Reid Melissa, PhD, Plax Katie, MD, and Drake Brett, PhD. "More Than Poverty — Teen Pregnancy Risk and Reports of Child Abuse Reports and Neglect" *The Journal of Adolescent Health.* (2015);

57(2):164-168. DOI:10.1016/jadohealth.2015.05.004. Article.

65. Livingstone, Amy, *Financial Benefits of Marriage vs. Being Single — What's Better?* Money Crashers. https://www.moneycrashers.com/financial-benefits-marriage-single/. Article.

66. Ibid.

67. Looney, Adam, *5 facts about prisoners and work, before and after incarceration.* Brookings Institute. (2018). https://www.brookings.edu/blog/up-front/2018/03/14/5-facts-about-prisoners-and-work-before-and-after-incarceration/. Article. Web.

68. Ibid.

CPSIA information can be obtained
at www.ICGtesting.com
Printed in the USA
LVHW050239291019
635545LV00003B/711